WRITING FO

'A brilliant series – an abs
tangible terminology and in
The books' methods and ta
teachers, and the clear, eva
obtain the necessary reflecti

Kesner Ridge, Hag
Outstanding

'This is the series we've all
objectives, these books pro
study. Whether your school
and/or Language to 6th fo
difference to results.'

Routledge A Level English equip AS and A2 Level students with the skills
they need to explore, evaluate, and enjoy English. What has – until now – been
lacking for the revised English A Levels is a set of textbooks that equip students
with the concepts, skills and knowledge they need to succeed in light of the way
the exams are actually working. The *Routledge A Level English Guides* series fills
this critical gap.

Books in the series are built around the various skills specified in the assessment
objectives (AOs) for all AS and A2 Level English courses, and take into account
how these AOs are being interpreted by the exam boards. Focusing on the AOs
most relevant to their topic, the books help students to develop their knowledge
and abilities through analysis of a wide range of texts and data. Each book also offers
accessible **explanations, examples, exercises, summaries, suggested answers**
and **a glossary of key terms**.

The series helps students to learn what is required of them and develop skills
accordingly, while ensuring that English remains an exciting subject that students
enjoy studying. The books are also an essential resource for teachers trying to create
lessons which balance the demands of the exam boards with the more general skills
and knowledge students need for the critical appreciation of English Language and
Literature.

ROUTLEDGE A LEVEL ENGLISH GUIDES

About the Series Editor

Adrian Beard was Head of English at Gosforth High School, Newcastle upon Tyne. He now works at the University of Newcastle upon Tyne and is a Chief Examiner for AS and A2 Level English Literature. He is co-series editor of the Routledge Intertext series, and his publications include *Texts and Contexts*, *The Language of Politics*, and *The Language of Sport* (all for Routledge).

TITLES IN THE SERIES

The Language of Literature
Adrian Beard

How Texts Work
Adrian Beard

Language and Social Contexts
Amanda Coultas

Writing for Assessment
Angela Goddard

Transforming Texts
Shaun O'Toole

WRITING FOR ASSESSMENT

Angela Goddard

Routledge
Taylor & Francis Group

LONDON AND NEW YORK

First published 2003 by Routledge
11 New Fetter Lane, London EC4P 4EE

Routledge is an imprint of the Taylor & Francis Group

© 2003 Angela Goddard

Typeset in Galliard by Keystroke, Jacaranda Lodge, Wolverhampton
Printed and bound in Great Britain by TJ International Ltd, Padstow, Cornwall

British Library Cataloguing in Publication Data
A catalogue record for this book is available from the British Library

Library of Congress Cataloging in Publication Data
A catalog record for this book has been requested

ISBN 0–415–28626–3 (hbk)
ISBN 0–415–28627–1 (pbk)

CONTENTS

TABLES

PREFACE

ASSESSMENT OBJECTIVES

The AS/A2 specifications in English are governed by assessment objectives (or AOs) which break down each of the subjects into component parts and skills. These assessment objectives have been used to create the different modules which together form a sort of a jigsaw puzzle. Different objectives are highlighted in different modules, but at the end of AS and again at the end of A2 each of the objectives has been given a roughly equal weighting.

Particular assessment objectives that are focused on in this book are:

English Literature

AO1: in writing about literary texts, you must use appropriate terminology

AO4: you must provide independent opinions and judgements, informed by different interpretations of literary texts by other readers

AO5: you must look at contextual factors which affect the way texts are written, read and understood

---

English Language and Literature

AO1: you must show knowledge and understanding of texts gained from the combined study of literary and non-literary texts

AO6: you must show expertise and accuracy when writing for a variety of specific purposes and audiences, and you must explain and comment on the choices you have made

---

HOW TO USE THIS BOOK

This book will be a useful text to work with at a number of different points in any course.

Chapter 1 highlights the fact that students need to be able to write in a range of different ways. This has practical outcomes: the PASS sheets in the chapter are used as a literacy log, to record and organise academic work. This chapter is useful as a starting point for any course in order to help set up a good culture of work practices.

Chapters 2 and 3 systematise what can appear as a new form of language to be learnt in its own right: the language of essays. This is not something that can be simply applied right at the end of a course, as a kind of optional add-on to exam revision. Trigger words for essay writing specify particular genres such as outlines, analyses, explanations and explorations. Each of these has its own rules and organisation, which need to be understood from the beginning.

Chapter 3 offers substantial analytical material for both language and literature that can be self-marked. After some initial use, these chapters will also, of course, be useful to return to at the end, as revision before examined assessments.

Chapters 4 and 5 focus on genres that are at the core of much work in English and beyond: investigation and argument. These genres are seen as being both ongoing approaches to work and particular assessment points. Both chapters offer analysis of how these genres work and then models for writing. Chapter 4 contains a wide range of language and literary data for investigation; Chapter 5 includes a journal article that can be used both for content and structure.

Each chapter contains a number of exercises. When the exercise introduces a new idea, there will usually be suggestions for answer immediately following. When the exercise checks to see if a point has been understood, suggestions for answer can be found at the back of the book.

ACKNOWLEDGEMENTS

The author would like to thank the following copyright holders for permission to reproduce material in this book:

Extract from *California Fire and Life* by Don Winslow published by Century. Used by permission of The Random House Group Limited.

Tall Stories: The Metaphorical Nature of Everyday Talk by Angela Goddard, in *English in Education*, Vol. 30, No. 2, 1996.

Two advertisements for The AA Driving School: 'LRN 2 DRV' and 'You only need one driving school to pass both tests', reprinted by permission of the AA. These advertisements are for study purposes only. Any offers may have ceased since the printing of this study text. Automobile Association Developments Ltd., 2001.

Children's writing in Figure 1.1 is from Tameside Primary Working Party, LINC Project: Tameside, Manchester and Stockport Consortium.

AUDITING YOUR WRITING SKILLS

CHAPTER 1

The aim of this chapter is to get you thinking about the way your own writing skills have developed, and about the particular types of writing required of you on your English course. In an ideal world, these two factors – your own writing abilities, and what your course requires – would be perfectly matched. However, in the real world it may be a different story: your course may prioritise certain types of writing you are less familiar with, and downplay some aspects that you know well.

By the end of the chapter, you will be in a position to know which types of writing are a strong part of your **repertoire**, and which types you will need to practise further. Make notes as you go through each exercise, in preparation for your Personal Audit Sheets (PASS) at the end of the chapter.

Exercise 1 – Your Writing Repertoire

Every individual has a range of writing styles, or repertoire, to select from according to the needs of a particular context.

Make a list of all the types of writing you have done in the last week. For each type of writing you identify, specify who the audience was and also say what the (main) purposes were. When you have finished, write some notes about how easy or difficult you found each type of writing.

There are no answers to this exercise, but what you do here will form the basis of further work to follow.

Table 1.1 is a brief example to get you started. It is from a young lecturer in his first year of teaching:

Table 1.1 List of writing types

Type of writing	Audience	Purpose
email	brother	information/entertainment
memo	work colleague	to record an agreement
notes for a lecture	self	to act as a prompt to memory

Notes on difficulty

The lecture notes were the most difficult to write because I'm new to this activity and I found myself having to do several things at once. For example, I had to look up quite a few references. I had to get my ideas into a logical order. I was writing with a view to how the lecture would sound when delivered, which meant that I had to think about such things as how long it would last. So the writing was really writing-to-be-spoken.

The memo was a little tricky because although it didn't involve much text, I had to get the wording absolutely right because the writing was going to act as a permanent record.

The email was the fastest piece of writing that I did and enjoyable because I included lots of stories about what's been going on. It did involve quite a lot of shaping of the text because I wanted to get maximum effect for some of the things I was describing, but I wasn't too bothered about correctness. I found the writing a relaxing experience which put me in a good mood because I could imagine my brother laughing as he read it.

The previous exercise will have shown you some of the factors at work in your own repertoire, for example:

- That you already have an extensive knowledge of different types of writing
- That you practise some types of writing more often than others
- That some types of writing pose more of a challenge than others
- That difficulty is sometimes simply the result of unfamiliarity
- That difficulty can arise from the need to use a particular type of language
- That difficulty can arise because one piece of writing may have to address more than one audience or purpose

You were probably also aware as you worked on the previous exercise that you could divide your writing into types that were to do with your social life and leisure activities – for example, text messaging friends in order to meet up – and types that were more associated with academic work, such as notes and essays.

Types of academic writing such as essays and reports are sometimes described as if they were acquired late in life, added on to an individual's writing repertoire after all the other types of writing, such as stories, diaries and poems, have been learnt. Actually, this is not true at all. Young children, if given the opportunity, will go way beyond just producing story forms. They are perfectly capable of constructing reports and accounts of the world around them that are quite analytical. This is because the thinking that lies behind some of the writing we call *academic* is actually a basic, everyday kind of thinking.

Exercise 2 – Early Repertoires

Read through the children's writing in the four texts below.

In what ways are these young children (all aged 5–6) being academic?

When you have finished the exercise, check the suggestions for answer on these texts at the back of the book.

The children had been working on a theme based on 'materials'. Much of this had been in the form of scientific investigations in order to find out about different types and uses of materials both natural and man-made. Towards the end of the half-term the teacher had asked the children to choose one aspect of the topic they particularly enjoyed in order to report back their findings to children in the adjacent Year 1 class.

Christopher

reel bricks sink and pleasteic bricks floak .on wakep.and thay flau BeCoS thay are noG hevy and reel bricks afe hevy-

Transliteration:

```
Real bricks sink and plastic bricks float on water and they float
because they are not heavy and real bricks are heavy.
```

Figure 1.1 Children's writing

Annie

We can yasie paPPe For
writ ing paPPe and
news paPPe and paPPe
of RaPing paPPe and
BOOKS of paPPe.

Transliteration:

We can use paper for writing paper and newspaper and paper of
wrapping paper and books of paper.

Figure 1.1 *continued*

ThingsabawtClos   Kelly

I wer clos to s&ool   ahd I wer clos to
Mg Threhs and I wer cloze eo The Parck
and a weding and I wet Themat hoem
ahd I wer Themat Wedings.
Poley esert and penim bnecotonahdacr.
allthe merris 7o clos

Transliteration:

I wear clothes to school and I wear clothes to the park
and a wedding and I wear them at home and I wear them at
weddings. Polyester and Denim and cotton and acrylic all
the materials of clothes

Figure 1.1 *continued*

The children made ice cream and observed changes of state as it was made and frozen. When reporting they each had to think of three changes that they had observed.

Jonathan

When we put The
chocolate Chips
in The pan
it went all
browny

When we put
The ice cream
in The freezer
it went solid

when The milk
were in the pan
it smelled
like ready brek

Jonathan

Transliteration:
```
When we put the chocolate chips in the pan it went all browny
When we put the ice cream in the freezer it went solid
when the milk were in the pan it smelled like ready brek
```

Figure 1.1 *continued*

The children's writing you have been studying arose because teachers were encouraging their pupils to attempt genres other than narratives (stories). The fact is, your own writing profile – your skills, the gaps in your knowledge – is the result of those writing experiences you have had, both within formal education and beyond. If you feel ignorant of some ways of writing, it could be because you never had a reason to practise particular styles with any regularity.

Exercise 3 – Language Across the Curriculum

Think in some detail about your own writing development, focusing particularly on the types of writing you did earlier in the school curriculum or on previous courses. Make some notes as you go along on each of the questions below.

Think first about the writing you did in English classes:

- What different types of writing have you previously done for English work?
- Of the different types of writing you did, which did you like most/least, and why?
- Can you identify types of writing that you did well, and types where you struggled?
- What were the most frequently expressed comments by markers about your writing in English?

Of course, it isn't only in English classes that students do written assignments. Now think about the types of writing you did for other classes:

- Give some examples, from other subject areas, of types of writing you did that were different from those you did in English
- Were you aware of learning different forms of language use in those other subject areas?
- Were you successful or unsuccessful at particular types of writing in other subject areas?
- Ask your teaching staff whether your school/college has any policies on literacy and language use across the curriculum (for example, policies for particular Key Stages or Key Skills). If so, identify what the school/college aims are for your literacy development

Exercise 4 – Literacy for Assessment

Get hold of a copy of the course description or exam board specification for the course you are on, and make a list of the different types of writing you are going to be assessed on. Below are some common assessment vehicles, but you may well find others. Tick those that apply to you, noting details for yourself of where the assessment occurs (e.g. end of unit exam, coursework, a particular unit or module, etc.). Then add any further examples you find. When you have finished the list, write a definition for each example of writing that you will have to produce, explaining what makes each written genre distinctive from the others:

- Logs
- Diaries
- Reports
- Commentaries
- Short answers – e.g. text analysis
- Research projects/investigations
- Essays

Some suggested definitions are given at the back of the book.

ACADEMIC LITERACY

It is impossible to talk about academic writing without also talking about academic reading. In order to understand how texts work, people need to become acquainted with a variety of written texts. Reading and understanding the material produced by a particular group are also a way for new members to become integrated. Think, for example, of any of your interests or pastimes, and the extent to which you have become familiar with the writing produced on that theme: if you like cookery you might read cookbooks and food columns; if you like football you might read fanzines and match write-ups; if you like shopping you might read magazines and catalogues. It is then likely that, if asked, you would be able to produce a piece of writing that was convincingly close to one of these **genres**, because you will have read them so often.

The same idea is true of the academic community. Those people who succeed in producing academic writing will have encountered many examples on which to base their own language choices – options both to follow and, equally important, to reject. This involves active reading, thinking and note making. And, although this section is termed 'academic literacy', which technically refers to reading and writing, you will see that written language is also supported by the oral work you do.

There are many types of academic material that can play an important role in supporting your own academic writing. Here are some:

- Teachers' oral presentations
- Teachers' written notes
- Class discussions
- Newspaper articles
- Textbooks
- Journal articles

All the genres above can contribute to your development of a good academic style. The oral genres – your teachers' oral presentations and your group discussions – are instrumental in developing your knowledge and clarifying your thinking. However, if you don't summarise in writing what was said, you will forget everything very quickly. Get into the habit of pausing to write down some brief summaries of points made in oral sessions. If you make a note of the date of the session, then you can reference any comments made in a professional way in your own writing (see Chapter 5 on how to reference). If you have never tried to write down anything in this way and have problems initially, then ask if you can record the session. Take the tape away and run it through at home, practising how to select points and summarise them in writing.

Newspaper articles, and other, similar, pieces of data such as magazine articles and webpages can be useful in a number of ways, particularly for reference to specific ideas and occurrences. This may be a matter of straightforward information (for example, the number of different languages in use in a community, the use of particular dialect words, an author's biographical details), or evidence of public attitudes to language, such as an editorial on the use of swear words or an arts column reviewing a recent play. You might well not agree with any of the opinions in the material you collect, but that doesn't matter: it will all be useful for you to refer to in framing your own argument. If you cut an article out, make sure you make a note of the date of the publication. You will need this for purposes of reference (see Chapter 5). If the article you collect is very long, write a short summary for yourself, and pick out one or two useful quotations. File any material you collect in a way that is logical to you.

Teachers often give out notes that they have made themselves, in order to help students with the work of structuring their ideas on a topic. These can be extremely useful, providing you understand what has been written. If you don't understand how the ideas fit together – ask. Teachers are generally pleased if you do this, as it shows you are making an effort to work things out. A frequently used method of teaching is for the teacher to give out a series of headings in the form of written notes, then talk about each of them. If this is the case, make sure you write down in your own words some explanatory notes to expand each of the headings.

Textbooks and journal articles (research papers written by academics) vary considerably in their level of difficulty and in who they see as their prospective audience. Some textbooks, such as this one, are specifically aimed at students; others are addressed more to other academics. If textbooks are collections of essays by different writers (such collections are sometimes called Readers), you may well find that some sections are more accessible than others. You don't have to read and understand every word in textbooks, but you do need to make notes on what you read. Making notes is an acquired skill that you will develop with practice. Remember to keep accurate details of the author's name and book or article title. Getting such basic details wrong makes you look sloppy.

PERSONAL AUDIT SHEETS (PASS)

In this final section, you will bring together your findings from all the work you have done in this chapter. Fill in the sheets that follow, which can function as a record of your writing skills at this point, and as a workplan for how you intend to move forward in developing your literacy. You could have a fresh sets of sheets for each term of work, if you wish: these sheets are downloadable from the Routledge website http://www.routledge.com/rcenters/linguistics/series/raleg.html

PERSONAL AUDIT SHEETS (PASS)

Name: Group:

Subject: Level:

Exam board and specification:

Units to be taken: on (date*):

*Specify dates of examined units and deadlines for coursework submission.

PERSONAL AUDIT SHEETS (PASS)

Types of writing required in the units are as follows:

Unit: Type of writing:

Assessment of my writing repertoire:

I feel reasonably confident about the following types of writing from the list above:

I feel less confident about the following types of writing from the list, which I will need to practise further:

PERSONAL AUDIT SHEETS (PASS)

Academic literacy development plan

Record details below of resources, including relevance to particular units or topics of work:

Taught sessions:

Date   Relevant to unit/topic/set book

Library resources (textbooks, journals):

Author, publication date, title   Relevant to unit/topic/set book

PERSONAL AUDIT SHEETS (PASS)

IT resources (e.g. CD-Roms, websites):

Title/website address	Date used/ accessed	Relevant to unit/topic/set book

Print media (newspapers, magazines):

Title/Nature of resource	Date	Relevant to unit/topic/set book

Visual/oral media (TV, film, video, radio):

Title/Nature of resource	Date	Relevant to unit/topic/set book

Other resources:

Nature of resource	Date	Relevant to unit/topic/set book

SUMMARY

In this chapter, you have:

- Considered the idea that you have a repertoire of writing styles
- Thought about how academic thinking and writing develop
- Explored how your writing skills have developed in the past
- Audited your skills at this point
- Planned to use and record a range of resources to develop your literacy further

UNDERSTANDING ESSAY QUESTIONS: TRIGGER WORDS

CHAPTER 2

One of the main reasons writers fail in essay writing is because they do not follow the instructions given. Sometimes, writers don't follow the instructions because they have pre-learnt an essay format which they are determined to write, regardless of the question set. But equally, failure can result because writers genuinely misunderstand what they are being asked to do.

Before you can start to plan any piece of writing, you need to understand the task set. Although thinking through what is required is the essential first step for any writing task, this task is often more difficult where essays are concerned. This is because essay questions often contain a language of their own, so they have to be translated before you can begin. The aim of this chapter is to focus on the language frequently used in the instructions for essay writing, so that you can feel confident in knowing what you are supposed to do.

WHAT IS AN ESSAY?

The essay format is often associated with presenting an argument. Although this is a common type of essay, and not an easy one to produce (see Chapter 5 for more detailed coverage), essays come in many other guises. For example, you can be asked to write a description of something, or to explain something. Describing and explaining are different from arguing, and different from each other, too.

In summary, the essay can cover many different types of work. What links these types of work together under the umbrella heading of 'essay' is the format itself. Essays typically involve:

- A presentation of knowledge and ideas
- The grouping of knowledge and ideas into paragraphs of related points
- The use of linking expressions to connect sentences and paragraphs together
- Formal openings and conclusions
- Writing in fully explicit sentences (i.e. not in notes)
- The use of standard English
- Adherence to formal rules of spelling and punctuation
- Reference to the ideas of others via quotation (see Chapter 5)
- A complicated notion of audience which is explained on page 16

In essays, you are not writing for yourself, but you are showing what you know and think. In this sense, an essay is proof that you have studied a set area or text, regardless of whether you are writing an exam answer or a piece of coursework. You are offering the proof of your knowledge and ideas to an examiner, but you are not likely to be informing them of things they do not know. Course booklets often advise students not to think of their tutors or examiners as their primary audience, but to think of a member of the general public who is interested in the area they are writing about but not an expert in it.

It may be best to use an analogy to explain the audience for an essay, and one which highlights the idea of performance. Imagine that you are on a stage, and you are performing to a crowd of people who are interested enough to come and see your work. They have bothered to turn up and they have paid some money, so they must be committed. They deserve a good performance from you.

While the crowd in the theatre stalls are your primary audience, there is another audience – a tutor or examiner – who sits in the wings and marks you on your performance. Your tutor has coached you along and got you to the point where you can go out onto the stage and perform on a regular basis. But on some occasions, you're on your own and in the lead role.

This way of viewing essay writing might sound a little far-fetched, but it's not that removed from the original meaning of the term, which is derived from the Old French word *essai*, meaning a 'courtroom trial', and connected with the Latin *exigere*, meaning 'to weigh'. Ideas about weight of evidence and about public performance are still significant in our modern concept of essay writing.

THE TRIGGER

At the core of essay questions are key words and phrases which give you instructions on what type of essay to write. These words are often known as 'triggers', presumably because they *trigger off* a certain kind of writing structure. Below are some examples. See if you can add any further examples to this list:

describe	consider	comment on
explain	analyse	give an account of
account for	define	outline
illustrate	assess	discuss
evaluate	compare	investigate
distinguish	state	summarise
contrast	interpret	review
justify	relate	judge
explore	write about	examine
imagine	identify	show
indicate	demonstrate	criticise/critique

Although this list may appear to contain a bewildering number of different types of instruction, it is possible to group some of them together as directing you towards a certain kind of activity. For example, the following terms are all asking you to say what things are like:

describe	outline	give an account of

Exercise 1

To see what kind of instruction these triggers are asking for, do a short piece of writing which attempts to describe/outline/give an account of the structure of your school or college day.

If you need to think of an audience, imagine that your account is for the school/college prospectus.

Now compare the triggers you have been using with these others, below:

assess	evaluate	analyse

These terms are not asking you simply to describe what happens or what things are like, but are asking you to take a step back from the experience and adopt a more critical stance, for example, by judging what the strengths and weaknesses of something are.

Exercise 2

Re-read the piece of writing you did for the previous exercise.

Now substitute one of the new trigger words above for the terms you acted upon previously, so that your task now becomes:

> Assess/evaluate/analyse the structure of your school or college day.

Write an answer to this new question. If you need to think of an audience, you could imagine that your school/college board of governors are thinking about making changes to the working day and want some users' views on the subject.

When you have finished your piece of writing, compare what you have written with the first piece of writing you did, for Exercise 1. What differences are there, and how do you explain them?

In reality, it would be unlikely that in an assessed piece of writing you would be asked simply to 'assess' or 'evaluate' or 'analyse' something, without being given a specific aspect to focus on. Question setters try to encourage writers to address the question in as specific a way as possible, and targeting a particular dimension can help sharpen a writer's response. This also has the effect of drawing a boundary around an area, making the answer easier to mark. So, for example, imagine that rather than just analysing the structure of the school/college day, you were asked to pay particular attention to one or more of the following aspects:

- The length and timing of breaks
- The number and length of taught sessions
- The amount of staff and student free time
- Start and finish times, including the possibility of twilight sessions
- The possibilities of online and offsite working by both students and staff

In this case, you might well be able to make your comments much more analytically focused than the one you wrote when you were simply asked to *analyse*. So, a more tightly worded question might now read as follows:

> Analyse the structure of your school or college day, with particular reference to the possibilities of online and offsite working by both students and staff.

By now, you should be starting to see why assignment and exam questions often appear rather long-winded: it is the result of question setters trying to structure the **focus** and **scope** of your answer. When questions appear as a long instruction, though, you need to develop the ability to see how many different parts they are composed of.

HOW MANY PARTS?

What looks like two sets of instructions in the question above is, in fact, one instruction where the words 'with particular reference to' define the focus for your attention and scope of your coverage. Here is the question again, modified by a phrase (written in italics) that changes each time. Read these through to get a sense of how they differ:

> Analyse the structure of your school or college day, *with particular reference to the possibilities of online and offsite working by both students and staff.*
>
> Analyse the structure of your school or college day, *with particular reference to start and finish times, including the possibility of twilight sessions.*
>
> Analyse the structure of your school or college day, *with particular reference to the amount of staff and student free time.*

> Analyse the structure of your school or college day, *with particular reference to the number and length of taught sessions.*
>
> Analyse the structure of your school or college day, *with particular reference to the length and timing of breaks.*

If you were really writing one of these answers, it would be unwise to confine yourself absolutely to the focus in a way that precluded any links with other aspects. For example, the possibility of online and offsite working would clearly have a big knock-on effect in terms of the start and finish times for the school or college day. Each instruction wording, then, is not forbidding you to mention other, related, aspects. But what it is saying to you is this: make the particular issue referred to the primary focus of your essay.

The question we have been examining has consisted of one instruction that is trying to help structure the answer by adding modifying phrases. This type of instruction is very common, but can appear differently according to how forcefully the advice for structure is expressed. For example:

> refer to
> you must refer to
> make sure you refer to
> you are advised to refer to
> in your answer you should refer to
> you may wish to include some or all of the following
> you may include any of the following, as appropriate

These modifying phrases are all subtly different. While the first one above is absolutely dictating what should be there, the last one is hinting that you shouldn't refer to everything on the list of items. 'As appropriate' really means 'make some choices here'.

Sometimes questions do not simply have one trigger, with or without some modification. Triggers can occur in the plural, even within one sentence in a question. For example, think about the two exercises you did earlier. Exercise 1 asked you to provide an outline, while Exercise 2 asked you to be analytical. It would be possible to combine these in one instruction, and even add a modifying phrase at the end as well. It would read something like this:

> Outline and analyse the structure of your school or college day, with particular reference to the possibilities of online and offsite working by both students and staff.

This question is asking the writer to present two different, but related, sorts of writing in their answer: an outline and an analysis. As you saw in your earlier exercises, an outline is a description of what something is like, while an analysis picks out significant features to be scrutinised in a more judgemental way. A marker of answers to the question above would expect to be given a general sense of how the school or college day worked, then a more detailed account of whether, given that structure, staff and students would be able to work online and offsite. The reader might be told, for example, that for online and offsite work to happen, the structure would have to change considerably. While the first part of the question above is concerned with the 'what' of the subject, the second part is more concerned with 'what if'?

For a question to have two parts in the way we have just seen, the two triggers have to be very different kinds of words. It would be a very poor question that asked the writer to repeat exactly the same activity. So the first words in the column below could all be paired with the second, because the first triggers are asking about what happens at the moment, while the second triggers are asking for something more complex – an exercise of judgement which could take many different forms including, for example, speculation on what could happen, consideration of the positive and negative aspects of situations, offering projected alternatives, and so on:

Table 2.1 Possible trigger pairings

Trigger 1		Trigger 2
outline	and	analyse
describe	and	assess
give an account of	and	evaluate

In the list above, trigger words for analysis will always follow those for description, not just because description is a simpler activity, but because description often forms the basis from which judgements are later drawn. You could think of description as setting out the territory for what comes later.

In Table 2.2 on page 21, the pairings are asking for the same activity twice – either description twice, or analysis twice. Hopefully, you will never find questions like these, although there is always the possibility of question setters having an off day. If you do find questions like these and you are in a situation where you can ask for clarification, you should do so, explaining that you appear to be being asked to do the same thing twice.

Table 2.2   Unlikely trigger pairings

Trigger 1		Trigger 2
outline	and	describe
describe	and	give an account of
give an account of	and	outline
assess	and	evaluate
analyse	and	assess
evaluate	and	analyse

Exercise 3

Focus on a topic or set book that you are studying or have studied in the past.

Compose a question on this topic or set book, and offer three variants of it as follows:

1. Write an instruction using one trigger word only.
2. Write an instruction using one trigger word but with an added modifying phrase, such as 'with particular reference to', which tries to narrow the focus and scope of the answer.
3. Write an instruction using two trigger words.

If you are in a situation where you can get some feedback, exchange your variant questions with those of another person, and see if you both understand what is being asked in each case.

COMPARATIVES

There are some specific trigger words that have the idea of partnership built into them as part of their meaning. For example, if you are asked to 'compare', you know just by the meaning of the word that you are going to be referred to more than one item. A similarly plural focus is implied by the word 'contrast'. The difference between these two words appears on the surface to be quite profound, with 'compare' suggesting a focus on what is the same, and 'contrast' suggesting a focus on what is different. For example, imagine that you get the following instructions:

- Identify a neighbouring school/college. How does the structure of their institutional day compare with yours?
- Identify a neighbouring school/college. How does the structure of their institutional day contrast with yours?

Actually, what you can probably see from the above variants is that their scope is slightly different, with the trigger 'contrast' suggesting less room for manoeuvre than 'compare'. In the first variant, although the main focus would be on what is the same, referring to how the two establishments differ would also be allowed. This is because saying how they differ would in effect show the limit of their similarity. Imagine that you were describing how you compared in terms of your physical appearance with one of your parents or relatives: you might say, 'Well, we look alike in this way and this way, but there the comparison stops because we are quite different in other ways.'

On the contrary, the term 'contrast' asks much more specifically about only what is different. If, in answer to the second question above, you discussed difference only after a long consideration of similarity, the relevance of your answer would be severely questioned.

This information should give you some insight into the thinking of the question setter: if they themselves think that x and y are very different, they are likely to use the term 'contrast'. If they want a major focus on shared elements but are happy to allow discussion of difference, they might well choose the term 'compare'. If they can see similarities and differences in equal measure and want to make explicit to you that you should bear both in mind, they are likely to use both triggers. For example:

> Identify a neighbouring school/college. How does the structure of their institutional day compare and contrast with yours?

There are, of course, other terms that encode ideas about similarity and difference: for example, 'relate' and 'distinguish'. Rather than expressing explicit instructions to compare and contrast, these terms suggest a looser general notion of connection and disconnection.

'Relate' carries the sense of bringing elements into a relationship, and you can see here not only that 'relate' and 'relationship' are connected derivationally (from the Latin word *relatum*, meaning 'brought back'), but that the storytelling meaning of 'relate' shares the same umbrella, too.

'Relate' is often used where question setters want to make sure a connection is made. For example, you might see as part of a question something like the following:

> Relate your comments to ideas from research

The opposite of relate, 'distinguish', tends to be used where items are easily confused and the question setter wants to know whether a learner has appreciated the difference. For example:

> Distinguish the term 'accent' from 'dialect'

WH- WORDS

It shouldn't be surprising that wh- words play an important role in academic questions, because they are at the basis of our ordinary questions in everyday life.

Wh- words are as follows:

> what
> why
> when
> where
> who
> how

Of these, the most frequently used words in written essay questions are 'what', 'how' and 'why'. These words may be small, but they are very significant. And they are very different from each other.

The word 'what' was used earlier in this chapter to explain the meaning behind the terms 'describe', 'outline' and 'give an account of', which were all seen as asking what something was like, or what happens. 'How' and 'why' do not ask about what happens, but rather about the mechanisms and reasons behind what happens. For example, think about the different meanings of the following:

> What happens in Shakespeare's *Romeo and Juliet*?
> How does Shakespeare tell the story of *Romeo and Juliet*?
> Why does Shakespeare summarise the plot at the start of *Romeo and Juliet*?

As you can see, 'how' and 'why' tend to set up more analytical questions than 'what', which in the examples above, asks for a paraphrase of the story. If the question concerned a theme or topic rather than a set book, 'what' could be an instruction not just for a description or an outline, but more condensed and abbreviated forms too, such as summaries and definitions. But, again, questions of how and why tend to be more complex than 'what'. Consider the following:

> What is 'political correctness'?
> How does 'political correctness' work?
> Why does 'political correctness' exist?

In the questions above, 'What is political correctness'? is asking for a definition, but the other two questions are asking more for explanations. In fact, you could use either of the alternative triggers for explanation – 'explain' and 'account for' – to replace 'how' and 'why' above:

> Explain 'political correctness'
> Account for 'political correctness'

As well as being used alone, wh- words have an important role in some specific phrases within questions, such as the following:

> To what extent do you agree?
> How far do you agree?
> How significant is this idea?

These phrases usually occur after a statement has been made, sometimes involving a quotation from a scholarly source. The phrases above are all similar because they all ask about the degree or amount of the writer's agreement or evaluation. They have an advantage over simply asking 'Do you agree?', or 'Is this significant?' in that they allow you to say that, in some respects, you don't agree with the statement or see the idea as significant. The same invitation – to say that your own views are complex, maybe even a bit contradictory – is set up by phrases such as the following:

> How do you respond?
> What is your response?
> What do you think?

Some of the trigger words that occur on page 16 of this chapter represent very different kinds of writing. We have seen already that while some words trigger descriptions – such as 'describe', 'outline' and 'give an account of' – others trigger analyses, such as 'analyse', 'assess' and 'evaluate'.

But there are also words that are associated with whole different genres of writing. For example, look at these from the original list:

Imagine	Discuss	Investigate
	Consider	Explore
	Comment on	

Not only do these entail different sorts of thinking and behaviour, but the activities they prompt tend to result in entirely different written genres.

'Imagine' asks the writer to put themselves in an *as if* situation that is likely to be different from the real world. This trigger tends to be used where question setters want to set up a context for writing. This may involve an entirely imaginary scenario – where, for example, the writer might be asked to construct themselves as a literary character. But it is a mistake to think that the word 'imagine' allows you to loosen all ties with social knowledge. For example, a good impersonation of a fictional character will offer very close references to what we already know about that character.

'Imagine' can also be the lead in to some very practically focused planning and writing. Many English specifications ask students to impersonate workers in cultural industries, such as theatre producers, arts journalists and copywriters. Here are some examples of this kind of task:

- Imagine that you are a producer who is hoping to stage a new version of Middleton's *Women Beware Women*. Your aim is to make the production as dramatically powerful as possible. Pick a particular scene and write a set of staging notes to indicate how you will use theatrical resources to enhance the actors' performances.
- Imagine that you are responsible for the pre-performance publicity for Middleton's *Women Beware Women*. Write a flyer advertising the forthcoming play.

In stark contrast, the triggers 'discuss', 'consider' and 'comment on' all tend to be associated with discursive writing of one kind or another, rather than the more creative productions imagined above. Like the very plain-seeming 'write about', these triggers appear rather vague when plucked out of context and just seen as single words. However, they often occur within particular kinds of grammatical structure where they are made more specific by the **object** of the sentence they are in. For example, imagine that you are the question setter for the second of the tasks above. You want students to produce the flyer, but you also want them to tell you about the decisions they made about what language to use. Your question might then appear as something like this:

Imagine that you are responsible for the pre-performance publicity for Middleton's *Women Beware Women*. Write a flyer advertising the forthcoming play, then comment on the language choices you made in planning and carrying out your writing task.

In fact, if this were a real exam question, the lines above would probably be split up in order to indicate a series of tasks, like this:

Imagine that you are responsible for the pre-performance publicity for Middleton's *Women Beware Women*.

1. Write a flyer advertising the forthcoming play.
2. Comment on the language choices you made in planning and carrying out your writing task.

More will be said about question layouts in the next chapter.

Exercise 4

Here are some more examples of triggers that may seem vague when used as single words out of context, but become much more direct in context. For each example, say how the words that surround the trigger help to direct the writer towards the task. Where there is more than one trigger used in a question, say how the triggers differ in what they are asking for, and how each trigger develops from the one before. In the original context, some questions had data attached to them. The data has not been reproduced here, but this omission should not cause you problems.

Some suggestions for answer to this exercise can be found at the back of the book.

Triggers:

> Comment on
> Explain
> Write about
> Discuss
> Consider

Tasks:

1. Read carefully Text B, which you will find below. It is a transcript in which the interviewee is a man from Bradford talking about his schooldays to a researcher.

   • Comment linguistically on the distinctive features of the extract
   • Explain how these language features contribute to the text's meanings

2. (A poem is printed in full on the exam paper)
   Comment on the poet's choice of verse form and language in this poem.

3. The following two texts are complete entries for the words 'man' and 'woman', both taken from the *Oxford American Dictionary* published in 1980.
   Write about some of the ways in which these definitions differ in their representation of male and female.

4. (With reference to Chapter 5 of Chinua Achebe's *Things Fall Apart*)
   Write about the way Achebe tells the story in this chapter.

5. (With reference to Jane Gardam's *The Pangs of Love*)
   Consider the use Jane Gardam makes of children in this and one other story.

6. (A number of extracts have been presented from pairs of set texts)
   Find the extracts from the pair of texts you have studied. Read them through carefully.

   Discuss the two extracts in detail, commenting on:

   • The ideas and themes and they ways in which they are presented
   • How the writers' language choices help to reveal attitudes and values

- What these extracts tell us about changes in language over time
- How far you think each extract reveals ideas, attitudes and values found in each text as a whole

7. Think of situations involving negotiating skills and discuss the role language plays in such contexts.

The exercise you have just done should have shown you that some trigger words rely heavily on what surrounds them for their instructional power. This is, of course, not true of all of them, as some triggers come ready-made with an approach already embedded in their meaning. For example, the trigger 'justify' carries a lot of directive meaning on its own. To go back to the question that formed the basis for Exercises 1 and 2 (page 17), think how different that question would be if set up as follows:

> Justify the structure of your school/college day

The term 'justify' asks for defence, for the writer to argue a case on behalf of someone or something. More will be said about argument in Chapter 5.

Finally, there is a group of triggers that appears to be used commonly in English exam and coursework questions because they suggest working on material. At the core of work in English, regardless of the specification being followed, is close analysis of how language is put together to form texts, both spoken and written. When candidates are asked to look at texts and say something about how they work, certain triggers become useful to direct those proceedings. For example:

explore	examine	investigate
indicate	demonstrate	show

You can see here that the three triggers on the top line above all share the meaning of 'have a look and see what's there'. The three triggers on the bottom line share a meaning, too – that of 'and point us to what you have found'. One trigger from each of the lines is a possible sequence in text-based questions: for example, 'examine the following text and show how language is used to create suspense'.

But a single trigger is also often used to suggest the two activities of scrutinising a text and writing up the findings. When a trigger is used alone, the assumption is that candidates will know there are two activities involved – researching and writing – because one cannot be done without the other. You cannot show what you have found without a careful trawl through a text; and you would be a very strange candidate if you had lots of findings but decided not to share them with the examiner. Here are some examples of the above terms used in context:

- Explore the ways in which Donne uses comparisons and contrasts in this poem
- Explore the connections between Act 1 and the rest of the play
- Show by detailed reference to the transcript how the speaker demonstrates specialist knowledge
- Examine the dramatic presentation of Malvolio in the play
- Indicate, by detailed reference to the text, how the two speakers present their attitudes and opinions
- Investigate the use of metaphor in this text, showing how it contributes to the text's meanings

Words such as 'exploration' and 'investigation' describe an activity you might other-wise call research. Obviously, if you are taking an exam paper involving set books, then you will have seen the material you are being presented with before, because that material will have formed the basis for your course. In that sense, you are hardly exploring the texts afresh. The same is true for some language study papers where, although the data itself may be new, the topic, subject for study or working method often is not. Exam-based textual analysis can therefore be slightly different from a more conventional research situation, where researchers often discover things that they didn't know before about material that is new to them. Nevertheless, triggers such as 'explore' and 'investigate' are there to remind candidates that the role of a text analyst is to dig around in the workings of a text and show its construc-tion. This, by its very nature, is a different activity from that of writing an argument essay.

Research-based terms such as 'investigation' are also used to describe work that does genuinely involve writing about new data and making discoveries, and many English specifications offer candidates the chance to put together their own enquiries, either in examined contexts or in ongoing coursework. Such activities tend to require a particular form of writing, and this will be addressed in detail in Chapter 4.

Exercise 5

1. Now that you have studied some trigger words in detail, you should be in a good position to analyse those used frequently in the assessments required for your particular specification. Look at some past exam papers and (if appropriate) some coursework titles students have used in previous years. Write some notes for yourself on the patterns of language used in the questions set. What do your examples reveal about the nature of the work that is expected for the units you are taking?

2. The topic of this chapter has been trigger words, but many of the same trigger words have been used in explaining what trigger words are. This situation has occurred because trigger words allow writers ways to instruct readers on how the material should be read. Go through this chapter and find all the trigger

words that have been used in the writing of it. What kinds of instructions have been given to you as a reader of this chapter? Did you see them operating at the time? Did you understand them? Did you do what they asked, or not?

There are no suggestions for answer to this exercise.

SUMMARY

This chapter has covered the nature of trigger words in essays, particularly:

- The difference between words for description and analysis
- How to analyse the number of parts in a question
- How triggers are modified
- Trigger pairings
- Comparatives
- Wh- questions
- Words associated with different genres of writing, especially imaginative writing, discussion and investigation

---

UNDERSTANDING ESSAY QUESTIONS: SECTIONS AND DIVISIONS

CHAPTER 3

When looking at trigger words in the previous chapter, it should have become evident that they do not operate alone. Much of the meaning of any question depends on how those words are modified – how they are combined with others. Although that is an important part of the way questions work, there is another element, too: how questions are divided and laid out on the page.

At first glance, this might seem more to do with issues of artistic elegance than meaning. However, you will see in this chapter that question layouts connect crucially with the nature of the task set. By the end of the chapter, you will have a much clearer sense of how to go about answering questions with multiple sections to them.

This chapter takes you through a range of different aspects of question layout and leads to an opportunity to practise what has been learnt.

WHY DIVIDE A QUESTION?

In the previous chapter, the following question was used to exemplify the trigger 'comment on':

> Imagine that you are responsible for the pre-performance publicity for Middleton's *Women Beware Women*. Write a flyer advertising the forthcoming play, then comment on the language choices you made in planning and carrying out your writing task.

It was then said that if this were a real question, it would most probably have been set out like this:

> Imagine that you are responsible for the pre-performance publicity for Middleton's *Women Beware Women*.
>
> 1. Write a flyer advertising the forthcoming play.
> 2. Comment on the language choices you made in planning and carrying out your writing task.

The reason for preferring the second of the layouts above is that splitting the question into clearly differentiated parts makes it clear that there are two distinct activities involved: writing a flyer, and writing a commentary on that flyer. If the question were written all in one go, there would be a danger that one or other of the activities would go unnoticed. You may think that you would never be foolish enough to miss out a whole activity because you hadn't read the question properly. However, the kind of reading that takes place in an examined situation is rushed because candidates know they are working against the clock. Question setters are eager to use any strategy that might help to clarify the question speedily.

Another strategy that is part of the preferred layout above is to separate the 'as if' situation and the reference to the text from the directions for writing. The trigger 'imagine' sets up an imaginary context where candidates have to think themselves into a role for writing. In separating this from the writing tasks, the message is that you need to take time to think about this role and give it some consideration before putting pen to paper.

A further device for dividing the question would be to use bullet points:

> Imagine that you are responsible for the pre-performance publicity for Middleton's *Women Beware Women*.
>
> - Write a flyer advertising the forthcoming play
> - Comment on the language choices you made in planning and carrying out your writing task

PROCEDURES AND THEMES

Regardless of which method is used to divide up the question, the important feature to notice about the particular thing we are looking at here is that you are expected to tackle each activity. The splitting of the task into sections is nothing to do with offering a choice, and everything to do with ensuring coverage. Because the second task has, by its very nature, to follow the first – you can't write a commentary on a piece of writing until you have done the writing – the sections form a **procedural** text. Procedural texts are those such as recipes and instruction manuals that involve a step-by-step structure where one activity has to be finished before the next starts, and where each activity is dependent on the previous one.

Rather than working procedurally, some questions go for a **thematic** approach, where the sections do not connect in a step-by-step fashion, but instead form composite parts of a picture. Here is a thematically organised question from the previous chapter. It uses a bullet point layout:

> (Pairs of extracts have been presented from several pairs of set texts)
>
> Find the extracts from the pair of texts you have studied. Read them through carefully.
>
> Discuss the two extracts in detail, commenting on:
>
> - The ideas and themes and the ways in which they are presented
> - How the writers' language choices help to reveal attitudes and values
> - What these extracts tell us about changes in language over time
> - How far you think each extract reveals ideas, attitudes and values found in each text as whole

The setter of the question above is indicating what needs to be covered in the answer. The fact that you are given the instruction 'comment on' rather than 'you may comment on any of the following', tells you, of course, that *all* the areas marked by bullet points have to be addressed. But one bullet point does not necessarily build on the one before. The various sub-themes must be explored in the texts, but you could start anywhere and finish anywhere.

Here is another example of a question where the sections are ordered thematically rather than procedurally:

> Explain the choices you made when writing your article by commenting on the following:
>
> - The content and structure of your article
> - Your choice of vocabulary and style in relation to your target audience

Again, in answering this question, you would need to cover the two specified areas, and there is a relationship between the two aspects: the subject matter or topic (bullet point 1) clearly has a connection with the style of communication used (bullet point 2). But the sections can be answered in any order.

USING THE STRUCTURE GIVEN

Aside from ensuring that all the specified areas are covered, the previous two questions you have studied do not instruct you to tackle their sub-sections in any particular order. Obviously, there is a natural order of events in some cases: for example, in the first question in this chapter, the flyer has to be written before the commentary. But many questions do not set up strict, sequential procedures that you must follow.

However, question setters often do imagine candidates going through their sections in the order in which they wrote them, and they do this because they often, perhaps even subconsciously, stage their sections in a way that they feel is **developmental** – that is, moving from relatively easy tasks towards those involving increased difficulty. Although, then, you are often free to tackle sections in any order, it would make sense for you to see whether the setter's plan is actually a useful one for you to follow. After all, why reinvent the wheel?

Here is an example of a setter trying to build a developmental structure for the candidate's answer:

> Read the following extract from *The Merchant's Tale* then answer all the questions.
>
> (Extract printed in the exam paper)
>
> 1. What do January's words reveal of his attitude to May and to marriage?
> 2. Comment on Chaucer's use of description and imagery in the passage.
> 3. How does Chaucer contrast youth and age in the tale as whole?

You don't need to know the tale or the extract concerned to see that the parts of the question above build from a smaller, easier focus towards a larger, more difficult one. (1) focuses on the words of a particular character in the extract; (2) casts the net a bit wider by moving back from a single character to ask about the writer's descriptive powers, but still within the extract; (3) asks about the way the theme of the extract is treated in the whole tale.

Question setters who are trying to stage an answer by moving from an easy starting point often ask a 'what-type' (i.e. content) question to start with, since 'what' is thought to be easier than 'how'. This is true in the Chaucer question above. Below are two further examples. Although the word 'what' does not appear in either of the first bullet points, the questions are still asking you to pick out items of content:

A recent newspaper article reported that Britain's police now have guidelines on what words and phrases they should not use, to avoid offending people or breaking the law:

- Give examples of words and phrases that you think the police and people in authority should avoid using
- Discuss the linguistic significance of your examples
- Discuss any alternative expressions that could be used

Read carefully Text B, which you will find below. It is a transcript in which the interviewee is a man from Bradford talking about his schooldays to a researcher:

- Comment linguistically on the distinctive features of the extract
- Explain how these language features contribute to the text's meanings

In each case, the question setter is offering a useful structure which moves from exemplification (*what*) to explanation (*how*).

BULLETS FOR CHOICES

So far, all the questions have involved obligatory aspects. None of the examples have offered a range of choices from which to select, but rather elements which must be included. However, some demarcating symbols – bullet points in particular – are also used to set up lists of items which are intended as suggestions.

In these cases, the activity is not to work through them one by one, but to treat them as hints from the question setter on what kind of thing to look for.

Here are two examples:

Do you think Russell's description of *Educating Rita* as a *comedy* is appropriate? You might consider, for example:

- Verbal humour
- Contrasts of character
- The play's structure, and its conclusion

(With reference to a radio interview)

Show by detailed reference to the transcript how both interviewer and interviewee demonstrate power and control in their discourse.

In your answer you should refer to any relevant research and also make use of some of the following frameworks, where appropriate:

- Lexis
- Semantics
- Grammar
- Pragmatics
- Discourse structure
- Phonology

Each case above is slightly different: the first question offers a small number of examples as starting points, while the second question offers a more extensive list from which to choose the most significant items. The language features that signal these different messages include the phrase 'for example' in the first question, which is shorthand for 'there are more possibilities but here are some to get you going'; and the words 'some' and 'where appropriate' in the second question, which mean 'don't go through the whole list'.

Despite having a slightly different slant, both questions are offering some guidance on what areas are likely to be relevant. Setters need to achieve a balance: they want to offer some help, but not make you think that the examples offered are the only ones to follow. Where they give very comprehensive lists, they want you to be able to make your own selections. In general terms, all question setters want to support but not inhibit.

Sometimes, setters explicitly tell you that their list is not definitive, by ending their list with an open-ended phrase. Here are two such examples, from questions on Arthur Miller's *Death of a Salesman*:

How do the play's settings contribute to its dramatic effect? You might like to consider:

- The home
- The garden
- Howard's office
- Other locations

Explore the ways in which stage directions and theatrical devices are used by Miller to create dramatic effect. You might like to consider:

- The stage directions for the opening act
- The use of music
- The woman's voice
- Anything else that interests you

You should read this kind of ending as a signal from the setter that they think the list is pretty open – that there are many further examples you could explore.

WHEN IS A CHOICE NOT A CHOICE?

The kind of speed reading done in timed situations can sometimes lead to mistakes because a slight change in wording can mean a large change in options. For example, look at the following phrases, used to introduce some of the bulleted lists above:

> you might consider, for example
> you might like to consider

In these phrases, the trigger word 'consider' has been modified by the **modal verb** 'might', which signals possibility: you are being invited to do something, not ordered to do it. Now look at the phrasing in the following set of instructions:

> (With reference to Chinua Achebe's *Things Fall Apart*)
>
> How important is story telling in the novel as a whole? In your answer you should refer closely to at least three stories that are told in the novel. You will need to consider:
>
> * Who tells the stories, to whom, and why
> * How the stories are told and what they are about
> * What the stories reveal of the novel's cultural background and how different readers might respond to them

In the introduction to the list, 'might' has changed to 'need'. Grammatically, the change is minimal, but semantically, the meaning is radically different. Think about the difference between the following utterances:

> you might like to go out for dinner
> you will need to go out for dinner

While the first is a suggested option, the second is a statement of necessity. In the question above, then, the setter is listing aspects that it will be necessary for you to cover.

You also have to watch subtle differences in expressions using the word 'select'. For example, the expression 'you may wish to select from the following' doesn't limit you strictly to the items on the list (but does suggest that the list contains some good choices). The instruction below, however, does not allow you to go beyond the list at all:

(With reference to Caryl Churchill's *Top Girls*)

How are the issues raised by the experience of two or three characters in Act One developed in the rest of the play? Select from the following:

- Isabella Bird
- Lady Nijo
- Dull Gret
- Pope Joan
- Griselda

HOW MANY EXAMPLES?

Surprisingly, questions asked in English often include references to number. Here are some quantifying words and phrases that occur quite frequently:

some
any
both
all
one or two
two or three
at least three

These terms occur in contexts such as the following, most of which have occurred in this chapter:

make use of some of the following frameworks
refer to any relevant research
both interviewer and interviewee
answer all the questions
refer to one or two poems
two or three characters
at least three stories

These quantifying words are important, the significance of their role often being shown by their being emboldened in the typeface of the question. Sometimes, this significance is about the mechanics of the task, and the way the task translates into assessed elements. For example, if a question asks you to answer three sections, covering two will earn you fewer marks than the possible maximum, regardless of how good your answers are. The same is true if you are supposed to consider both x and y: considering only x will earn you only half marks. But while phrases like 'all' and 'both' are fairly straightforward, what does 'at least three', 'one or two', or 'two or three' actually mean? Are these phrases evidence of question setters not being able to make up their mind?

One of the difficulties facing question setters is that they have to produce questions to suit a wide range of ability. Better answers often go into detail about a more limited range of material but there must be scope in questions for people who are less analytical to still show their best work. This can sometimes be most easily achieved by offering candidates the chance to extend the number of items they cover.

The logical conclusion to draw is that, if you feel able to analyse in a good amount of detail, you should go for the lower number in questions with numerical options: so, for you, 'at least three' will mean *three*. However, if you struggle to make analytical points when you are faced with a limited amount of material, go for the larger number and you will be able to score some more marks on the basis of coverage.

HOW MARKS WORK

You might think that marking is only something that need concern the markers of your work. If so, you'd be wrong. Information about the allocation of marks can help you to gauge how much time and effort to put into various parts of a question. It can also help you to understand to what extent you are free to repeat or overlap your ideas in any answer.

Exam papers vary in where they put their information about marking, but you will find some details if you look for them. The details are likely to be in one of three places:

1. On the front of the paper, or at the beginning of a new section of the paper. This option tends to be chosen when all the questions to follow carry equal marks.
2. At the end of each part of a question.
3. At the end of a whole question.

Options 2 and 3 above mean quite different approaches to marking are being taken, so you should tailor your answers accordingly. If marks are given for each sub-section, this means that you need to treat each of the parts as if they were separate from each other. In fact, this approach is only used where the parts are clearly distinct, so you shouldn't have difficulty in this respect. Here is an example, taken from earlier in this chapter:

> Imagine that you are responsible for the pre-performance publicity for Middleton's *Women Beware Women*.
>
> 1. Write a flyer advertising the forthcoming play. (50 marks)
> 2. Comment on the language choices you made in planning and carrying out your writing task. (25 marks)

Where this approach to marking is taken, points that are relevant to one sub-section but mistakenly put in another cannot be credited. However, the two tasks here are asking for quite different types of writing, so there is unlikely to be any problematic overlap. Note, though, that the two parts are weighted unevenly. If you spent most of your time on the second part of the question, you'd probably be wasting a lot of potential marks. Mark weightings always tell you something about how the question setters have estimated the demands of the task.

Option 3 is different from 2 in that, instead of giving each part a mark, a global figure is allocated for the question as a whole. This approach tends to be used where the sections of the question have a close relationship with each other. Here are two examples that were used earlier in this chapter, this time with some marks information attached:

Read the following extract from *The Merchant's Tale* then answer all the questions.

(Extract printed in the exam paper)

1. What do January's words reveal of his attitude to May and to marriage?
2. Comment on Chaucer's use of description and imagery in the passage.
3. How does Chaucer contrast youth and age in the tale as whole?

(30 marks)

A recent newspaper article reported that Britain's police now have guidelines on what words and phrases they should not use, to avoid offending people or breaking the law:

• Give examples of words and phrases that you think the police and people in authority should avoid using
• Discuss the linguistic significance of your examples
• Discuss any alternative expressions that could be used

(50 marks)

The setters here have been unwilling to credit each part with a separate mark, because each of the parts is closely interconnected. The advantage to you in this approach is that you can be credited for making a good point about any of the parts wherever that point happens to occur. You are free to go through the question one part after another, or to collapse all the sub-sections together and write one holistic essay.

The disadvantage for you in this approach is that you have no information about how long you should spend on each aspect. This is a very different situation from the task involving the publicity flyer, where you could translate the marks allocation into ideas about scope and timing.

In fact, there is some information to be gleaned just from your own thinking about the relative difficulty of the parts of questions. For example, in the question on *The Merchant's Tale*, the first part of the question is less demanding than the other two parts, because you are being asked to focus on a specific, small area and there is a limited amount to be said. It would therefore make sense to try to finish this part fairly quickly in order to allow yourself more time for the more demanding work where there is more to say.

The extent to which you can separate the easy parts from the harder ones will vary from question to question, but often, 'what' questions are easier to answer than 'how' and 'why' (see the wh- words section in the previous chapter). So, for example, if you are asked what a text is about and how it works, your realisation that the 'what' question is the easier part should give you the confidence to finish this part quickly and move on to the often more challenging questions about structure and techniques.

In analysing the parts of questions, though, you also need to think about how much of the more difficult area is dependent on the easier one, because you could finish a 'what' question quickly, only to find it coming back to haunt you. For example, in the parts of *The Merchant's Tale* question, the first area is fairly detachable: you are asked to focus on the words of a character and say what they suggest about his attitudes. But look again at the other question used above:

A recent newspaper article reported that Britain's police now have guidelines on what words and phrases they should not use, to avoid offending people or breaking the law:

- Give examples of words and phrases that you think the police and people in authority should avoid using
- Discuss the linguistic significance of your examples
- Discuss any alternative expressions that could be used

(50 marks)

In this question, superficially the first part looks easy: give examples. However, as you read through the other bullet points, you realise that a lot depends on this initial selection. You are unable to leave these examples behind, because the second bullet asks you to talk about their connotations, and the third to give possible substitutes. If you don't choose your initial terms thoughtfully, the whole essay will be weakened.

The more familiarity you have with styles of exam and assignment questions, the more expert you will become at understanding where setters think the meat of an answer is likely to lie. Sometimes, this is observable just through noticing the repetition of key words and phrases. For example, look again at the following question, used earlier in this chapter:

(Pairs of extracts have been presented from several pairs of set texts)

Find the extracts from the pair of texts you have studied. Read them through carefully.

Discuss the two extracts in detail, commenting on:

- The ideas and themes and the ways in which they are presented
- How the writers' language choices help to reveal attitudes and values
- What these extracts tell us about changes in language over time
- How far you think each extract reveals ideas, attitudes and values found in each text as whole

The setters are clearly interested in you telling them about what is in these extracts (and the whole books from which they are taken). You can see this from the use of 'ideas' and 'themes'. The terms 'ideas' and 'themes', like 'topic', and 'subject matter', relate to our 'what' question. However, the setters are even more interested in the 'how' question, in how the texts are put together and how they might be understood. This interest is expressed by the following phrases:

the ways in which they are presented
changes in language over time
attitudes and values (in the extract)
attitudes and values (in the whole books)

Noting the repetition of terms that relate to the 'how' question should, in this case, help you to realise that the bulk of your time and attention needs to be paid to how ideas are expressed in these texts.

THE STYLE OF ANSWERS

The discussion above was designed to get you thinking about how to use your time and energy economically when planning how to answer a question. You can economise further by troubleshooting some of the stylistic issues that will face you when you start to write.

Multi-part questions often look attractive because, as was illustrated earlier in this chapter, the different sections can form a useful structure for you in writing your answer. However, you still need to follow many of the conventions of essay-style writing. For example, in answering under headings, you may feel paragraphing is unnecessary because this has already been done for you. This is not true: think for a moment about the headings offered by this question, used earlier.

> Read the following extract from *The Merchant's Tale* then answer all the questions.
>
> (Extract printed in the exam paper)
>
> 1. What do January's words reveal of his attitude to May and to marriage?
> 2. Comment on Chaucer's use of description and imagery in the passage
> 3. How does Chaucer contrast youth and age in the tale as whole?

You don't have to be familiar with the text to realise that the first question asks about more than one aspect of January's attitude; and that there will be many points to make about the way Chaucer uses language and treats a particular theme. So in no way will sub-sections such as these function as paragraph headings. You will always need to group your points into smaller entities within the larger headings you are given.

Although you need to write in Standard English and not in note form, you don't need the formal openings and closings that may be familiar to you from essay writing in other contexts. In particular, you don't need to introduce texts or authors to your reader, whom you can assume has knowledge of the books and issues they are asking questions about.

Finally, questions that have sub-sections but a global mark for the whole entity need to be thought of as one complete effort. This means that where a point has been made early on, it doesn't need to be repeated for the later parts of the question. Assume that one person is reading the whole question, and will count your remarks wherever they occur. Remember, though, that this doesn't apply to questions where the parts have their own mark allocation. In this case, you need to treat each part as an independent element.

Exercise 1 – A Simulation

Choose one question from the choices below, and either write a timed answer as an exam simulation, or use the activity as the basis for a piece of coursework. When you have finished, check your answer against the suggestions for answer at the back of the book, and award yourself a mark. (Alternatively, if you are in a group situation, exchange work with a partner and mark each other's work.)

Question 1

Read carefully Texts A and B.

Text A is from the Yellow Pages; Text B is from Ford car magazine.

Answer all the questions.

(a) Compare and contrast the language of the two texts.

(b) What conclusions do you draw about the reasons for the similarities and differences you have identified?

In your answer you should consider:

- Grammatical and semantic features
- Aspects of layout and design
- Intertextuality

(50 marks)

Figure 3.1 Text A

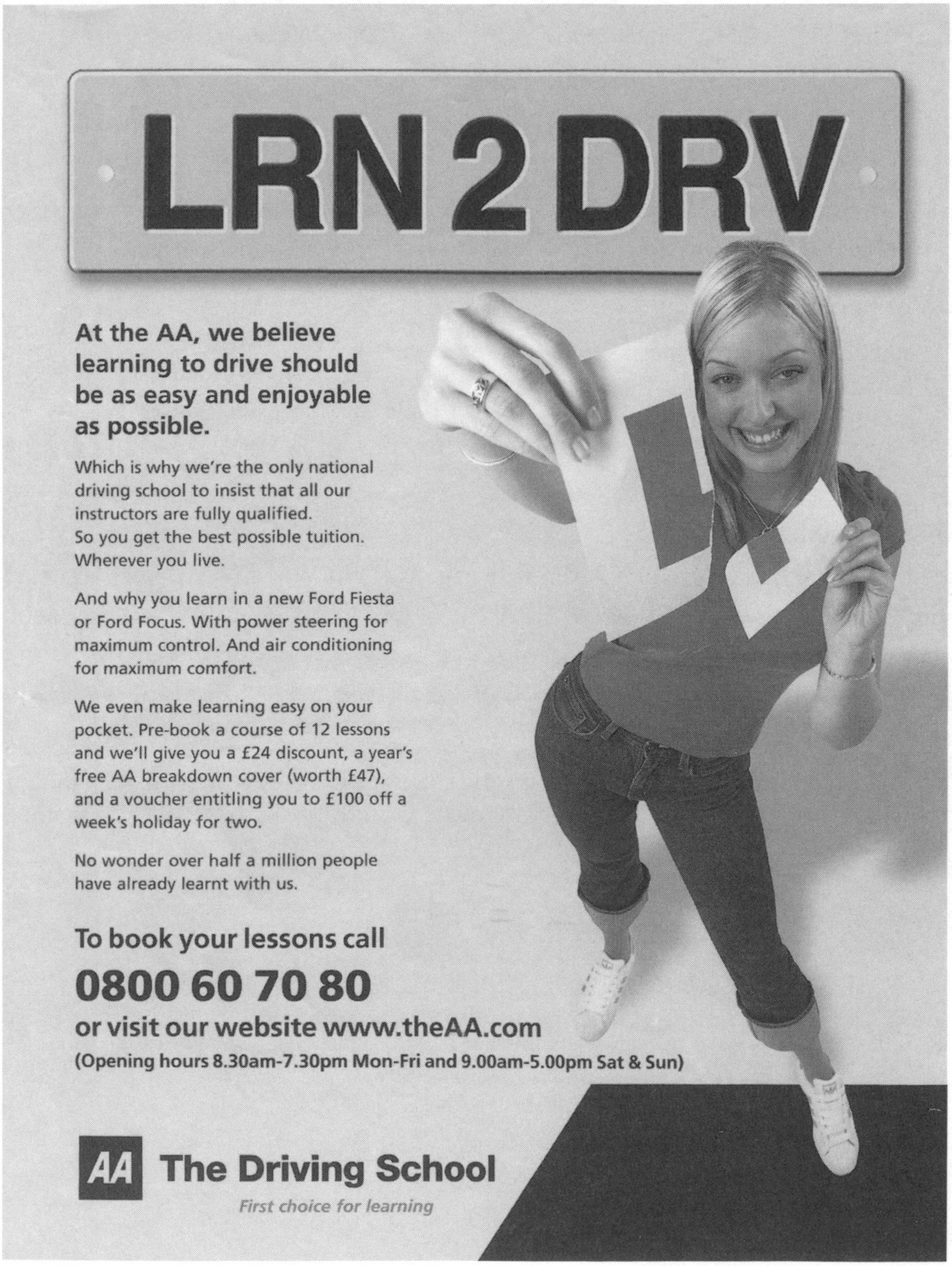

Figure 3.2 Text B

Question 2

Read carefully Text C, which is the first page of Don Winslow's detective novel *California Fire and Life*, about an arson investigator.

Answer both questions.

(a) What kind of work does a novelist have to do on the opening page of a novel?

(b) How does Don Winslow use language in order to do the work you have described above?

You will need to consider:

- Genre and intertextuality
- Point of view
- Grammatical and semantic features

(50 marks)

Question 3

Read carefully Text C, which is the first page of Don Winslow's detective novel *California Fire and Life*, about an arson investigator.

Answer both questions.

(a) Using this extract as a model, write your own opening page for a piece of detective fiction. (50 marks)

(b) Write a commentary which explains the language choices you made in planning and writing your text. Do not write more than 300 words. (20 marks)

Text C

1

Woman's lying in bed and the bed's on fire.
    She doesn't wake up
    Flame licks at her thighs like a lover and she doesn't wake up.
    Just down the hill the Pacific pounds on the rocks.
    California fire and life.

2

George Scollins doesn't wake up, either.
    Reason for this is that he's lying at the bottom of the stairs with a broken neck.
    It's easy to see how this might have happened—Scollins's little Laguna Canyon house is a freaking mess. Tools, wood, furniture lying all over the place, you can hardly walk across the floor without tripping on something.
    In addition to the tools, wood and furniture, you have paint cans, containers of stain, plastic bottles full of turpentine, cleaning rags . . .
    This is also the reason the house is a bonfire.
    Not surprising, really.
    Not surprising at all.
    California fire and life.

SUMMARY

This chapter has covered:

- Why questions are divided, and ways of dividing them
- Procedural and thematic questions
- How to use a question structure to build your answer
- How choices are offered or restricted
- Numerical references
- How marking works
- Aspects of style
- Practising your new knowledge and skills

INVESTIGATING

CHAPTER 4

The previous two chapters have focused on the way essay questions in general are constructed to produce a particular type of answer. You have seen how question triggers and formats are closely connected with distinctive forms of writing, such as descriptive outlines, textual analyses, definitions and explanations. This chapter and the next will look in more detail at two specific types of writing: investigation and argument. These genres feature frequently on academic courses in many subject areas, and often count for significant proportions of overall marks. Each genre represents a very different kind of activity, and each has its own specialist rules and terminology. The first genre to be considered will be investigation.

WHAT IS AN INVESTIGATION?

Like arguing, investigating is both something of an everyday activity and a specialist academic one. The term 'investigation' comes from a Latin word *investigare* which means 'to follow a track' or 'to trace something out'. Every time you consult a dictionary, look through a recipe book or ask another person about their experiences, you are being investigative, in the ordinary sense of the word.

Academic courses expect you to be investigative in your general approach to work. The Personal Audit Sheets you encountered in the first chapter of this book showed you that you need to notice, explore and record the resources around you in order to build up your academic knowledge of your subject and the skills to express your ideas clearly. Beyond this ongoing approach, however, there are particular points where you may be asked to conduct a formal investigation of a topic or text. In this situation, investigation means something very specific, involving several processes which culminate in a written report.

It is difficult to offer advice on how to write up an investigation without first doing the research itself. For this reason, this chapter will take you through the investigative process via some simulations. You will then see how the decisions you make about the writing of your report are closely connected with the kind of study you have set up for yourself.

GETTING STARTED

Investigative work is usually an opportunity for you to direct your own study. This means that you decide on an area for research, set up your own question, and carry out an enquiry before writing it all up. If you are doing this for a piece of coursework, it will involve you finding your own data. In an examined situation, data will of course be provided for you, but you still have to go through the other stages described above.

Before you start thinking about the endpoint of writing up your work, you need to break down the process of investigation and see its various stages clearly in your mind. This will help you to plan a structure for yourself, regardless of whether that structure has to fit into three months or three hours.

Below you will find a number of stages, with questions. Answering the questions for each stage will help you to structure the investigative process for yourself. Go through the questions and make sure you understand them, noting that sometimes questions are slanted differently according to whether you are doing coursework or an examination. You will be applying this structure later to some data.

THE INVESTIGATIVE PROCESS

Stage 1 Interests and Feasibility

Both exam and coursework

It is always better to choose something that will stimulate you and get you thinking in new ways, rather than play safe and go for something predictable. So, looking back over the course you have taken so far, which aspects and approaches have interested you particularly? Look again at the reading you have done: were there any examples of research in secondary sources that you could follow?

Coursework only

How feasible is it going to be to investigate one of these aspects? For example, you may be interested in something, but it is impossible to gather data on it.

Try to be realistic: think of an area you find interesting and for which data will be available. If you have never come across a certain type of research in your reading, it could be that no one has had the imagination to do it. On the other hand, it could be because the data is impossible to collect.

Exam only

Does the data you have been given include any of the aspects you found interesting on the course? If so, is there enough data for you to be able to discuss it in detail? Remember that in an exam you are not allowed to add your own data or go beyond what you are given in any way.

Stage 2 Draft Question

Establishing a rough idea of a question involves making some decisions about the focus and scope of your study. Focus and scope were discussed in Chapter 2 (see page 18). Focus is about which aspects will be given your particular attention; scope is about how much ground you will cover in the study. For example, in an area of language acquisition, your focus could be on the acquisition of telephone skills. Your scope could range from narrow – studying one child, studying just phone call openings – to a wider one involving several children and a whole range of different skills.

Arriving at even a draft question is likely to involve you in making quite a number of choices, and this applies as much to examined situations as to coursework. This is because, in examinations, you are often given more data than you need: your ability to be selective is therefore part of the test. Here is a checklist to use as a possible starting point for both exam-based tests and for coursework:

- Will you study spoken or written language, or both?
- Will you use a single text or person, or compare a number of texts/people?
- If you are using a range of texts, are they from one genre or more than one?
- Will you look just at contemporary usage, or historical changes?
- Will you focus on structural aspects, or functions, or both?
- How many structures/functions above will you cover?
- If you are looking at social groups, how many groups will you cover?

There is no set rule about how narrowly or widely you should frame your investigation, except that there are the obvious constraints of word count for coursework and time for examined papers. A general guide is that it is always better to go into detail about a smaller amount of material than cover a lot of data in a less analytical way.

Look back to the information in Chapter 3 about references to number (page 38), where there was some guidance on how to approach questions that allow you to define your own scope. This suggested that while it was preferable to achieve a detailed, narrow scope, it was still possible to score some marks by extending the coverage of an answer.

The same idea applies to investigations. The best approach is to offer a detailed analysis of a well-defined area but if you find working at that level of detail difficult, expand your coverage of aspects to enable you to say more.

Offering candidates of different abilities an opportunity to show what they can do sometimes requires question setters in investigation exams to be flexible in their wording. For example, you might see the following instruction:

State the aim(s) of your investigation.

As with the questions using number references in Chapter 3, this isn't an example of question setters being undecided about what they want. This is a coded way of saying 'If you can, focus on one aim and produce a detailed analysis of the data. If you can't do that, don't stick at one aim and say a small amount. Instead, choose more than one aim and say something about each aspect.'

In all your thinking about your research question, refer again to any reading you have done and look further to see if there are any new forms of reading you can do to support your work. Your investigation doesn't have to consist of something no one else has done before. In fact, some of the best research takes an idea approached previously and investigates it in alternative ways. Even doing exactly the same research again after a period of time has elapsed is a valid exercise.

Stage 3 Initial Data Collection

The stage above was labelled *draft* question because it is not until you've done some preliminary data collection and reviewed your material that you can decide on a final form of wording. Changing your focus as a result of what your data reveals is not a problem or a mistake: it is part of the learning and discovery process. For example, you might have decided to record some children using the telephone, but found that the adults they were talking to were doing some very interesting things with their own language. You might then decide to change the focus of your investigation from the language used *by* children to the language used *to* children.

Although in investigation exams you are not involved in data collection, you are involved in data sorting, which is likely to include several shifts of focus as you consider what is in the data.

In neither case are shifts such as that outlined above problematic, because they would be occurring during the process of investigation. When it comes to writing up your work, you will have chosen a route through the material you have collected or sorted.

In the case of coursework, undertaking some preliminary data collection has an added benefit – some insight into what the whole data collection task will involve. It may be, for example, that you had planned to record a certain kind of conversation, but it proves impossible; or that you had planned to collect some particular types of adverts or news articles or literary texts, but none of them are available; or that the effects you were interested in do not translate from real interactions into transcript form. Doing what amounts to a small pilot study can have many advantages, including diverting you away from unproductive routes and ensuring that your proposal falls squarely within your course specification guidelines.

Stage 4 Final Question and Data Collection

After your initial work, you should be in a position to make a firm commitment about what exactly you are going to do. At this point, you need to complete your data collection or selection, and start to think about what your data reveals.

Stage 5 Analysis

There is no single form of analysis that all investigations need to do. It all depends what you are hoping to discover. Your choice of methodology needs to be suited to the question you are exploring, and to the type of data you have collected or selected. For example, you may decide to explore public attitudes to dialect via questionnaires, while another student wants to know how a dialect poet uses language to express their ideas. Conducting the former investigation would involve you in some **quantitative** analysis, where, for example, you might add up the numbers of people who agree or disagree with certain statements. The latter investigation would be more of an interpretative or **qualitative** study focusing on one individual's discourse.

One type of analysis does not rule out another, however. In both the cases above, it might be a good idea to use a mixture of methods. For example, encouraging **informants** to express their ideas freely as well as answering the set questions in questionnaires can often enrich your results. On the other hand, counting the occurrence of dialect features in a poem can be a useful strategy to add further weight to an interpretation.

Whatever type of analysis you choose, you will always show the following:

1. What is in the data you have collected or selected.
2. The implications of what your data reveals.

The term 'implications' can, of course, mean many things: for example, the mechanisms used to construct a text (the 'how' question referred to in Chapters 2 and 3), or the possible reasons for people holding certain views (the 'why' question).

You do not need to know all the answers, but you do need to speculate on the nature of your material in as much detail as you can. Speculation in this context means setting out in writing your responses to what is in your data.

Your analysis is the core of any investigation, and the place where you earn many of the possible marks in assessment. In order to make the work of analysis more manageable, you will need to arrive at some headings under which you group points and deal in turn with the various aspects of your chosen topic. Although you will have been working closely with your supervisor throughout, making sure you check out your proposed headings with your supervisor is particularly important at this stage. Obviously, you cannot do this in an examined situation, but by the time you arrive at the exam, you will have experienced a number of simulations where you did check out your proposed headings for the analysis of sample material.

The headings you devise should bear a close relationship to your aims and the nature of the material you have collected. For example, a dialect study such as that described above, where public attitudes are being investigated via a questionnaire, will have asked a number of questions of informants. The headings for analysis would therefore need to be based on those questions. For the sake of illustration, these could be something like the following:

- Informants' definitions of dialect
- Informants' most and least favourite dialects
- The contexts suggested by informants for the use of dialects

Under each of these headings, you would present your results and discuss their implications.

Stage 6 Writing Up

After all your work to establish a research aim, collect/sort and analyse data, you need to write up the process you have been through in a way that will make sense to someone who has not been involved in your work. As with essay writing, it is probably best not to think of your supervisor or examiner as your primary audience (see Chapter 1), but someone who is interested in your topic without being an expert. The various sections you have in your write-up (both for coursework and in an exam) will depend on the nature of your investigation, but the following model is common:

Aim(s): a clear statement of what you were aiming to do.

Reading: any information that you have gathered from your reading which has helped you to think about your investigation and analyse your data. This will need proper referencing: see Chapter 5 for further information on this.

Methodology: how you collected/selected your data; also, an explanation for the reader of how the data will be presented and analysed in the next section.

Analysis and discussion: sections, with headings, indicating what you have found in your data, and what the implications are of your findings.

Conclusion: a brief summary of the most important points you have found.

Academic writers sometimes move between the present tense and past tense in research reports. If they do this, it is because they are following a particular tradition of writing which has grown up in certain academic areas. In this tradition, researchers sometimes behave as if they are taking the reader on a journey, getting the reader to experience the research as if, at least to start with, it is still happening. So they might say, for example, 'my aim *is* to explore . . .', 'I *will be* analysing . . .'.

At a certain stage, the researchers then move to the past tense, saying, for example, 'what I *found* was . . .'. It is important that you are aware of this style of writing because you may come across it in your reading, and therefore feel that you have to follow it as a model for writing. However, you need to make your own decisions about how best to communicate with your reader, and if it feels easier to you to write up your report all in the past tense, that is fine. Some people would claim that was more honest, anyway.

The important factor is that you give some thought to the whole process of communication. Your report must be readable and accessible. This entails not only thinking about how to present the steps you took in your investigation, but considering where your data is best placed for easy access by the reader. In exams, you should take advantage of the labels and line references you are given in order to refer to texts and parts of texts. If you are working on coursework, a well-established convention is to have your data in an appendix at the back. However, you might decide that for the sake of readability you want in addition to bring some material forward into the body of the analysis and repeat it there. You might also decide that some of your discussion is best presented in the form of graphs or tables, instead of continuous prose. There is no right or wrong approach: all these decisions are for you to make, according to the particular nature of your work.

Exercise 1

Return to the two texts in Chapter 3, advertising the AA Driving School.

Brainstorm some possible research questions for which these texts could be the data. Start by just focusing on these two texts alone, then consider how you might add further texts to the collection in order to be able to ask other research questions.

To help you think of further texts, use the Stage 2 checklist. Here it is again:

- Will you study spoken or written language, or both?
- Will you use a single text or person, or compare a number of texts/people?
- If you are using a range of texts, are they from one genre or more than one?
- Will you look just at contemporary usage, or historical changes?
- Will you focus on structural aspects, or functions, or both?
- How many structures/functions above will you cover?
- If you are looking at social groups, how many groups will you cover?

Use the bullet points to brainstorm all the different dimensions you can think of. For example, if you wanted to study the 'spoken' language of driving tuition, you would need to tape record some lessons, and transcribe them.

Some suggestions for answer are given at the back of the book on possible further texts and approaches. However, such a list will never be definitive, so if you have come up with something you do not find at the back, this doesn't mean you have gone wrong in your thinking.

Exercise 2

Return to the literary extract in Chapter 3, where the opening page of a detective novel is presented. How could you use this text as the basis for an investigation? Think of further texts that could be added to this one, and some different research angles that you could take.

Again, there are some suggestions at the back of the book, but they are not definitive.

Exercise 3

It was suggested earlier in this chapter that the analysis section is the core of any investigation, and that for an analysis to be effective, researchers need to be able to identify patterns of language use. It is therefore worth getting as much practice as possible in sorting data into analytical categories and attaching appropriate headings.

Read through the items below, which are the names of some schools offering driving tuition. They are from two different sources – *Yellow Pages* (in the Newcastle upon Tyne area), and a UK-based *Internet Directory*.

Group the names into categories according to the patterns of language use you observe in the data. Devise some category headings, and discuss the implications of the categories you find. Pay attention to any differences between the sources as well as similarities. You will find some suggestions for answer at the back of the book.

Write up your work formally, as the analysis section of an investigation into the nature of driving school names. Write a brief conclusion on your findings.

Data for Exercise 3

Source: *Yellow Pages*

1 Ace school of motoring
1st Ladydrive
EZYPAS SoM
1A Passmasters
Advance School of Motoring
Pass Mark Driving School
Able School of Motoring
1st choice quickpass driving academy
Academy Driving School
Bob Robson SoM
Bede driving school
Drivewell SoM
Drivetime
Calm drive

Ken Cooper SoM
Gosforth SoM
Green for Go
Driving Force
Sure Pass Driving School
Select Gear Driving
L-Passo School of Motoring
Karma school of motoring
Noel's driving school

Source: *Internet Directory*

website addresses (all had http, etc.):

bsm
intensivedriving
ldrive
passedyet
streetwise

Exercise 4

Read through the items below, which are the titles of a number of novels in the detective fiction genre. Imagine that this data has been collected by you from the detective fiction shelves of your local library in order to carry out the following investigation:

An investigation of the nature of detective fiction book titles.

Group the titles into categories according to the patterns of language use you observe in the data. Devise some category headings, and discuss the implications of the categories you find.

You will find some brief suggestions for answer at the back of the book as a starting point. They are not fully written up because you should now be aware of how to expand your notes into a discussion, as a result of working on the previous exercise.

Write up your work formally, as the analysis section of your investigation. Then write up the full investigation, following the 'write-up' model given earlier in the chapter. Don't forget to supply a brief conclusion.

Data for Exercise 4

Threatening Eye
Loverboy
A Long Line of Dead Men
Heartwood
Burning Angel
Blood Work
The Concrete Blonde
Trunk Music
Cruel and Unusual
LA Requiem
Dead Lagoon
Blood Rain
Cosi fan Tutti
The Church of Dead Girls
One for the Money
Final Jeopardy
Known Dead
Wasted Years
Easy Meat
Cold Light
Freezing
True Crime
Prayers for Rain
The Disposable Man
Scent of Evil
The Caterpillar Cop
Toxic Shock
M is for Murder
Night Passage
Thin Air
Walking Shadow
Mortal Causes
Let it Bleed
Set in Darkness
How the Dead Live
Certain Prey
Mapping the Edge
Quick before They Catch Us
Aftermath
Mystic River
Every Dead Thing
Dark Lady
The Big Sleep

God is a Bullet
Dark Hollow
World Without End
Sidetracked
In a Dry Season
Cutting Edge

Exercise 5

For this final exercise, do the following:

- Devise your own question
- Choose some data either by using all the material given, selecting only a part of it, and/or adding to it with data of your own
- Set up a range of headings for analysis, and do the analysis
- Write up your study using the model given earlier in the chapter, remembering to write a brief conclusion
- Write less than 4,000 words, excluding the data

There are no suggestions for answer provided for this exercise.

Data for Exercise 5

Below are two data sets, both of which involve language use and new technologies. The first data set consists of some emails sent by a number of different individuals in a college to a staff tutor called Margaret. The tag (+ *automatic signature*) shows you that in the original mails, the email programme automatically attached the writer's name and address.

The subject information for each email has been taken from the original subject line.

The mails have been numbered for easy reference.

```
Subject: funky editing!

Maggie,

I am sure that you will be delighted to hear that I have
obtained a set of guidelines for the production of a definitive
document. Needless to say they make reference to many mysterious
acronyms and processes of which I understand about 20%. I will
put a copy of said guidelines in your pigeonhole.

I have also got hold of someone else's attempt to come to terms
with this lunacy — ie. def. doc. from another course. I am
getting the distinct impression that this wont be a funky
editing job.

I think that it might be an idea if we could find a couple of
hours for an initial meeting so that we can begin to identify
what we dont know / understand and what jobs need to be done.
The sooner we can do this the sooner we can sort out who does
what from the rest of the team and take it to a meeting in the
near future

Yours in anticipation and excitement — Steve
```

Figure 4.1 Email 1

```
Subject: me

direct line 9796 884 2524
```

Figure 4.2 Email 2

```
Subject: Re: new course
Maggie
Graet stuff.
I'm free tomorrow between 10.00 and 10.30 or after 2.30.
Come to room 79 if your able.
Best,
JR
(+automatic signature)
```

Figure 4.3 Email 3

```
Subject: Re: tutorials
hi, sorry i didn't make it to the tutorial yesterday as i had an
important doctors appointment. by the time i arrived everyone
had left the lecture theatre. i understand that u were arranging
ono to one meetings with us yesterday. if u could fit me in with
ur arranged sessions it would be much appreciated. thanks...
kate x
```

Figure 4.4   Email 4

```
Subject: Re: where in Italy?
(no message in body of email)
```

Figure 4.5   Email 5

```
Subject: tutees

Hi Marge

Nice minutes — Stuart liked them alot!

I'm not sure if you know that Mike has additional tutees than
indicated on that initial list, I put another list in your p/h.

Sorry!

Also I would like to check out some dates to see if you're
around to keep an eye on my house — ie. US conference etc — but
I am going to go home and work this afternoon before coming back
in to meet up with some students for the evening — so if you
fancy a cuppa let me know as I will be going via Tesco's and
intend to but some thing nice to eat, like cake!

speak soon

Hxx

(+ automatic signature)
```

Figure 4.6   Email 6

The second data set consists of a number of answerphone messages left on the answerphone of the same person, Margaret Brown, by different callers.

Outgoing message:

Recorded message for incoming callers to hear:

Hello / this is 83845 224 360 / I can't take your call at the moment / please leave a message and I'll call you back

Message 1:

hiya just ringing to say the dreadful Sophia Mitchell got the job / so I should think I'm for the high jump / see ya

Message 2:

um hello Margaret / it's John Davies / I'm just ringing to confirm that somebody will be at the airport to pick you up / I think it's twelve fifteen / I haven't actually got my letter with me / I haven't got your letter with me / but whoever's going to pick you up will know it's you / and will be there at the right time / bye bye / see you on Friday

Message 3:

hi Maggie this is Emma / um / I can't make any changes to the article / because you've got the last version of the disk / or the last version / you did the changes on it / I believe / um / so there's no point me carrying on and doing any changes / so could you stick me the disk with that on in the post / and / um / you'll need to save it as / not probably the Word file that you've got / the Word file on the system that you've got / because mine's older / so it needs to be saved as an older version of Word / so my computer can read it / hope that makes sense / bye

Message 4:

hi Maggie it's Alison / I'm back from ski-ing and I had a brilliant time / if you get this can you give me a ring / I need to have a chat about next week/ thanks / bye for now

Message 5:

hello hello hello / are you there / obviously not

Message 6:

hi it's Helen / I'm just ringing up to say a happy Christmas / and all that kind of thing / and see how you are / and / um / I'm off I'm off to Ireland this week / but when I get back let's get together / and eat and drink and things like that / and walk maybe and do stuff / and all that kind of thing / so hope you're ok sweetie / and have a lovely time / speak to you soon / bye

Message 7:

hello / it's me just phoning to see how you're feeling / speak to you soon /
bye

Message 8:

hi Margaret / it's me / stop being an antisocial bastard / and give me a ring
/ and speak to you soon / bye

Message 9:

here's my message / give me a ring

Message 10:

hello / this is a message for Margaret Brown / this is Andrew at Blackwell's
bookshop / letting you know that the book you ordered has arrived / so you
can pick it up whenever it's convenient / thanks / bye

SUMMARY

This chapter has covered:

- The nature of investigating as an activity
- The idea that investigations can be broken down into stages of work
- How to brainstorm different research questions
- Choosing data
- The way analytical sections and conclusions can be structured
- Following a model for writing up a whole study

ARGUING   CHAPTER 5

This aim of this chapter is to help you develop the skills you need for writing argument essays.

It was said in the previous chapter that investigating was both an everyday activity and an academic one. The same is true of arguing. Whether you're consciously aware of it or not, you integrate into your daily routines such activities as the following:

- Putting forward your point of view
- Questioning what you are told
- Contradicting people
- Offering evidence for a claim
- Asking someone to justify their position

All these activities are part of the behaviour we call 'argument'. Here is a dictionary definition of this behaviour:

argue. give reasons or cite evidence in support of an idea, action, or theory, typically with the aim of persuading others to share one's view.
(The New Oxford Dictionary of English 1998)

Just as academic courses expect you to learn how to be investigative, they also expect you to learn how to argue a case in an appropriate way. This is different from being argumentative. Being argumentative is wanting to argue just for the sake of it. The ability to argue a case is more about discovering what others have thought, deciding what you think, and learning how to express your views in a reasoned way.

Exercise 1

Although there are connections between everyday forms of argument and academic argument essays, the language used to express ideas in those contexts is somewhat different. While all forms of argument make references to 'evidentiality' – presenting claims to truth and questioning others' claims – there are many ways to handle evidence linguistically. For example, look at the terms below. These are all from *spoken contexts* where people are engaged in argument.

- Can you add to this list any other words and phrases that are used in *speech*?
- Explain what speakers are trying to do when they use terms such as these
- How many of the terms could be used in *written* forms of argument?

mark my words	mind you	and another thing
so what?	how come?	that's rubbish
it stands to reason	I'm not being funny, but . . .	don't get me wrong
to be fair	at the end of the day	it strikes me that
well, if you ask me	I'd just like to say	to my mind

There are some suggestions for answer on these terms at the back of the book.

This exercise should have helped you to see that although we can argue both in speech and in writing, the language use in those contexts is different. There are clearly some terms that belong much more comfortably to the spoken mode than the written one.

Although you will need to make sure you don't write too informally in argument essays, it is a mistake to go to the other extreme and assume that argument essays require an extremely formal style. You need to write clearly and straightforwardly, but you don't have to scour the thesaurus to find complicated items of language in order to sound academic.

ARGUMENT TRIGGERS

It is possible for you to be given the word 'argue' as a trigger in its own right. A question instruction could go something like this:

Argue the case that metaphors are used in everyday language, as well as in literature.

This question is asking you to adopt a particular position, and put that forward as strongly as you can.

There are other triggers that could be used to ask you to do the same thing. For example:

Justify the view that metaphors are used in everyday language, as well as in literature.

Although the question immediately above does not use the word 'argue', it still presents you with a position to take up and asks you to support it. Other similar, triggers could include phrases such as 'make a case for'.

The terms above are very clear signals that arguments are expected. But there are also less obvious phrases that ask you to present a view. These phrases often appear as part of a question sentence. For example:

> to what extent . . .?
> how far . . .?
> do you agree?
> what is your response?

These phrases ask you to set out an argument, but with a difference. Rather than the absolute agreement that is expected by terms such as 'justify' and 'argue the case that', the phrases above allow for more concessions to other points of view.

The first two phrases above will tend to appear at the front of a question. Here are some examples:

> To what extent do metaphors occur in everyday language, as well as literature?
>
> How far do metaphors occur in everyday language use, as well as in literature?

The final two phrases from the list will tend to occur after the question has been fully set out. For example:

> It is sometimes claimed that metaphors occur in everyday language, as well as in literature. Do you agree?
>
> It is sometimes claimed that metaphors occur in everyday language, as well as in literature. What is your response?

A further way of asking you to present your views is to set out a question and then to use the trigger 'discuss'. This is perhaps an older form of question setting, often using a quotation from a scholarly source. Don't be misled by the use of the word 'discuss' in this context. It really is asking you to present an argument. Here is an example:

> 'Research has been discovering that our everyday discourse is highly metaphorical' (Goddard 1996). Discuss.

THE STRUCTURE AND STYLE OF ARGUMENT ESSAYS

Once you have established that you need to write an argument, you need to think about how an argument is structured – in other words, about its overall shape or genre.

The write-up of an investigation is a 'report' or 'account' genre, where activities are described in the order in which they happened. This is the genre that you saw in its early form in Jonathan's report of ice-cream making (see page 6). Argument structures are not based on a time frame in the same way. Argument is much more about the linking together and grouping of ideas into themes. In an early form, you saw this in the writing of the other young children (see pages 3–5), where there were attempts to classify and make general statements, sometimes with justifications.

Written argument is sometimes referred to as **expository** writing, meaning writing that 'sets out a position'. In order to set out a position, you need to have some knowledge of an area, and, again, you saw this form in the early writing samples. The children had gained some knowledge – of paper, of clothes, of building materials – and their writing was expressing that knowledge in particular ways. Your PASS sheets are a running record of the knowledge that you are acquiring.

Unless you are specifically asked to present the pros and cons of an issue, you should think of argument as a way of presenting one main position and holding it, while also showing that you are aware of other views. There is a subtle, but important, difference between being aware of other views and agreeing with them. If you appear to agree with every point on every side, your writing will be a mess and your reader won't have any idea what you really think.

The report genre you studied in the form of an investigation write-up had something of a ready-made structure because it followed a process of discovery, and this created headings for analysis. Argument structure is less automatic, and will obviously depend on what is being proposed. But argument essays do need to be **cohesive**, moving on from one point or theme to the next in a logical order, so that the reader can follow your line of thinking. For this to happen, you need obviously to have your points grouped in note form before you start to write, but when you do write, you need to make sure that you signpost to the reader how you are moving from one aspect to the next. An important signposting device is the first sentence or **topic sentence** of a paragraph, which should act as a link with the ideas that have gone before. Often, topic sentences relate directly to the ideas in the previous paragraph.

In the case of the opening paragraph, a topic sentence might briefly tell the reader what the writer intends to do. It is important not to write a long introduction, though, because before you know it you will have spent all your time and words explaining what you are going to do rather than actually doing it. It is worth noting that you never need to write out the question as your starting point.

Exercise 2

Read the text below, which consists of the first ten paragraphs of a journal article. Journals are collections of academic articles by different people. Each article will have the following introductory features:

Title of the article
Details of authorship
An abstract, which is a summary of the ideas or argument being proposed
Key words, for use in electronic searches

At the bottom of the pages, you will find further details of the journal: its name and issue details (in this case, *English in Education*, Vol. 30, No. 2, 1996), and the academic group that organises the publication (in this case, the National Association for the Teaching of English).

Do the following:

1. Read the abstract carefully. What ideas do you get about what you are going to read in the article?

2. Find each topic sentence and explain how the words and ideas in it relate to what has gone before. In the case of the opening paragraph, explain how this sentence gives some indication of what is going to happen in the article. Each paragraph has been numbered, for easy reference.

There are some suggestions for answer on this exercise at the back of the book.

Tall Stories: The Metaphorical Nature of Everyday Talk

Angela Goddard Centre for Human Communication,

Senior Lecturer in English, Centre for Human Communication, Manchester Metropolitan University

Abstract

This article questions some popular cultural assumptions about the nature of everyday discourse. It claims that such discourse is in fact richly metaphorical and that, through the operation of metaphor, we fictionalise ourselves as we talk. Because literary writing has dominated our culture and curriculum, English teachers have not been encouraged to explore an aspect of language that is at the core of how we think and behave.

Key words

Spoken English, metaphor, everyday discourse

1   This article is called 'Tall Stories' because in it I want to look at some of the stories we have in our heads about what talk is like, and ask whether they're true or not. More particularly, I want to question one of the tallest stories we have in our culture about talk – and that is that the everyday variety is a transparent medium, a bit of a metaphor-free zone.

2   In fact, research has been discovering that our everyday discourse is highly metaphorical, and metaphorical in systematic ways that relate to the way we think and behave. In order to show this, I want to look at the nature of the metaphors we use as our common currency, and ask some questions about what our everyday metaphors say about us – what stories do they tell about us?

3   You'll have noticed that I've already used a number of metaphors: tall stories; 'looking at' metaphor; talk as a zone; talk as money; and metaphors as people. The metaphors I've used so far represent two very common metaphorical strategies that we use every day – abstract as concrete (ontology), and thing as person (personification).

4   The fact that I managed to use five metaphors in four sentences via two different metaphorical strategies without this being particularly marked makes two important points about what talk is like: first, it's a lot more difficult than you might think to talk to people without recourse to metaphorical structures; second, we don't notice our everyday metaphors until someone points them out, or until the structures break down. There was a nice example of breakdown recently when a Radio 4 journalist, talking about how difficult it was to prove that Mark Thatcher was involved in military arms sales, said 'so here we're really trying to nail down a bad smell, then'.

English in Education, Vol. 30, No. 2, 1996

5   While we go on not noticing our own everyday metaphors, and while we stick to the idea that talk is a rather unembellished form of communication, we gasp in wonder and delight at the metaphorical complexities of literary writing. Why is this?

6   To unpick this question (I've noticed that women tend to unpick issues, while men tend to unpack – you can draw your own conclusions about that) we need to think about how we conceptualise our subject of English itself, because that's very relevant to why people might have difficulty thinking that everyday talk is metaphorical. This idea goes against the received wisdom we have about talk, which is that it is somehow straightforward and serviceable – a bit like Marks and Sparks underwear, hard-wearing but not particularly sexy, getting us through life without major mishap. We don't associate metaphor with this function: metaphor for most people, including most teachers of English, I would say, means literature – language with a designer label on it.

7   These representations are part of a larger picture we have evolved about English – that there is a division of the subject into 'language' and 'literature'. This division is very strange, because literature *is* language, after all. It's a bit like saying that in your shopping basket you have vegetables and carrots. We have this division as the result of our cultural luggage (another nice metaphor there, and maybe the reason why men do so much unpacking). This luggage tells us that literature, as 'the best words in the best order', is *the* subject of study within English, with the development of language skills being associated with perceived low-level uncreative functions, like clerical tasks.

8   You still see these ideas reflected in descriptions of courses, and in analytical frameworks: literature and language are often ranged along a continuum where the variable is the factor of creativity, so that language at its extremity is often exemplified as something like the minutes from a meeting (this being our idea of language at its most languagy), with literature at its extremity being, often, poetry (our idea of literature at its most literary, and the place where most of us would probably locate metaphor if asked).

9   Through polarisations of this sort, then, we have apparently constructed a number of damaging oppositions, setting literature against language in a rather crude 'plus and minus' fashion – what one has, the other hasn't. Creativity is one of these oppositions, but there are other dimensions too: for example, the idea that language is a vehicle for information while literature isn't; that language has fixed meanings operating on a single level, while literature generates fluid, multi-level interpretations – multiple readings, with readers bringing different ideas to texts. And we've generated a whole industry from the latter idea within literary study.

10   In the end, though, historically we've convinced ourselves that much of ordinary language – particularly talk – is really not very interesting because of its transparency of meaning and its generally unremarkable, uncreative, formulaic nature. So we certainly don't see everyday talk as being the home of figures of speech (even though we call them figures of *speech*) like metaphor.

Exercise 3

Now read the rest of the article, which is printed below in an edited form. Then do the same activity as you did previously: identify each topic sentence and explain how it relates to what went before. The paragraphs continue to be numbered.

There are no suggestions for answer on this exercise.

11   With the advent of some useful technology, however, things are changing fast on the talk front, not only because of the nature of tape recorders, but also because of the ability we now have to compile corpora of spoken language on computers. By using computer-based data, we're now in a position to start drawing up archives – as we already have for writing – of descriptive rules for spoken discourse. Speech grammars, in other words.

12   Clearly, many different types of text are needed to account for our speech behaviour, and it's worth just thinking for a moment about the kinds of archive that we need, and that, in some cases, are starting to emerge: first, we need some descriptions of spoken grammar in the sense of the structures which repeatedly vary on the basis of our big demographic groups – region, ethnicity, gender and so on; second, we need some descriptions of the spoken structures we all use, regardless of group membership – features such as repetition, hedging, backtracking, fillers and reinforcers, hesitations, trailing off, and other aspects of what Crystal and Davy (1969) called 'normal non-fluency features'. Once we have the latter, we'll be able to quash once and for all the way notions of correctness in writing have been applied to speech, as if either the two channels were the same, or speech were a corrupt form of writing. We also need descriptions of our speech behaviour in a wider sense – discourse rules and discourse variations.

13   What we also need, of course, is some decent mapping out of our semantic system, and such a mapping would give metaphor a prominent place. We don't have this yet in language study, but it's something that linguists working in semantics have been working on for some time (for example, Lakoff, 1987; Lakoff and Johnson, 1980). Our existing dictionaries are not particularly helpful here, because they treat language as single items, and don't provide an account of the way we organise our vocabulary conceptually. What conceptual accounts would try to do is open up the thinking and ordering that lie behind our simplest use of words and phrases, showing systems of meaning.

14   For example, one large group of metaphors we operate with are those that I referred to at the start as 'ontological' – that is, they talk about abstract entities as if they were concrete. This is clearly a very powerful facility to have, because we would be very limited communicators if we could only refer to concrete and observable things. One set of abstracts we deal with every waking moment are our emotions. We don't know where they are, we can't see them, but we can feel them and experience the results of them.

English in Education, Vol. 30, No. 2, 1996

15   A very common metaphor we use for the relationship we have with our emotions is to see our bodies as containers and our emotions as substances within them. To illustrate this idea you only have to think of the way we metaphorise one emotion – for example, anger – and track it via language output. We have something like the following system:

1. The body is a container, and anger is a boiling liquid:
    Anger welled up inside me.
    I was seething (an old word for boiling).
    I was spitting with rage.
    I was bubbling with anger.
    I just boiled over.

2. The body is a container, and anger is fire which can set the container alight:
    I was burning with anger.
    I was breathing fire.
    I started fuming.
    Smoke was coming out of my ears.

3. The body is a container, and anger is an explosive substance which can blow the body apart:
    I exploded.
    I just blew up.
    I just went off (specific: volcanoes – she erupted; electricity – she blew a fuse).

4. When the container explodes, parts of it fly off and become projectile:
    I flipped my lid.
    I blew my top.
    I hit the ceiling.
    I went through the roof.

5. The body is then out of control:
    I went crazy.
    I went out of my mind.
    I lost it.

16   When you think about these phrases, they seem perfectly transparent and logical on one level – that is, when you experience anger, it feels as though it's gathering force inside you – and you can see why we might think of ourselves as containers. We are physical beings with a bounded surface, and we must be conscious of ourselves on a day-to-day basis as delicately contained by the skin that separates us from each other and the outside world. In a real sense, we must be worried about ourselves spilling out.

English in Education, Vol. 30, No. 2, 1996

17   But you could also argue that the language we have constructs our reality too – that we view our emotions in a certain way *because* of the language that we have. This idea – of the shaping influence of language on thought and behaviour – is a longstanding one, and you often see it described as 'the Sapir-Whorf' hypothesis (named after two American linguists, Edward Sapir and Benjamin Lee Whorf). The following extract sums up the position they took:

> *. . . we dissect nature along the lines laid down by our native languages. The categories and types we isolate from the world of phenomena we do not find there because they stare every observer in the face; on the contrary, the world is presented in a kaleidoscopic flux of impressions which has to be organised by our minds – and this means by the linguistic systems in our minds . . .* (Whorf, 1956)

18   How does this work with our anger metaphors? Well, if we metaphorise ourselves as the container, and our emotions are a substance within the container, then we are saying that our emotions are not us, so it's an easy step from there to saying that we cannot be held responsible for them. If you take an analogy, it's like saying we are a saucepan and our emotions are the soup inside the saucepan. If the soup boils over, you don't blame the saucepan – you blame the source of the heat.

19   For a practical example of the effect of this type of metaphor, you don't have to look very far in the discourse of rape trials to find men described as if they shouldn't be expected to be in control of themselves, with women often blamed as the source of the heat. So, when looking at the way metaphors construct reality, we need to ask: whose metaphors are they? Who do they construct reality for?

20   Ontological metaphors such as the 'anger' series are commonly found in descriptions of behaviour. Here what we often do is to account for complex patterns of behaviour that we find hard to describe, in terms of behaviour that is more tangible and definable. Consider relationships, for example: desire is hunger (I'm hungry for you); the object of desire is food (he's tasty); relationships are journeys (we've come to the end of the road, you go your way, I'll go mine, we're at the crossroads); argument is warfare (I got picked off and sniped at, he shot himself in the foot and went off at half-cock).

21   Everyday metaphors such as these illustrate the fact that language is not simply a way of describing an idea, but the way we talk is the way we construct our norms of social behaviour. At the strongest point of connection, you could say that the way we talk is the way we act: the language *is* our behaviour, we behave in a warlike way when we argue. At the weakest, you could say that the metaphors describe a set of norms to us, which we see as the framework to follow. In other words, we may see the 'relationships are journeys' metaphor as an ideal – if our relationships don't measure up to this metaphor, we feel a failure.

22   But are these metaphors useful, and are they the only way to think? You can see the logic of them in some ways, but in other ways they may construct a

English in Education, Vol. 30, No. 2, 1996

damaging picture for us too. For example, if desire really is like hunger, then we're giving ourselves a hard act to follow – after all, we eat several times a day and we expect a lot of variety. If relationships are like journeys, then we must feel that we ought to have a destination in mind, plus, presumably, a sense of constantly changing horizons. And is taking an aggressive and oppositional stance really the best way to sort out an issue in an argument? Is war a good model for anything?

23   What if we saw relationships as sculpture, and argument as dancing? How would we behave then? This is the point where you really begin to see what it means to be a member of a cultural group, and the part that so-called ordinary language plays in constructing a sense of group identity and reality. Our metaphors can look very 'natural', particularly where we feel they have a physical base, as in the many orientational metaphors we use: for example, happy is up, sad is down, the future is ahead, the past is behind. But even these metaphors are not universal: there are languages in which the future is behind and the past is in front. The past is in front because you can see what's already happened; the future is behind because it's as yet unknown – and it has a nasty habit of springing alarmingly over your shoulder one day and becoming your present.

24   It's clear that metaphor, used in everyday discourse, is a powerful human communicative facility. However, because metaphor so pervasively structures our everyday reality, it shapes our experience and behaviour in ways that are easily overlooked. To treat metaphor as if it's some ornamental addition to language that only appears in literary contexts is to describe the language feature wrongly. To see it as the sole province of literary authors downgrades ordinary speakers and also doesn't show how literary authors fashion a universal resource in new and clever ways.

References

Crystal, D and Davy, D. 1969. *Investigating English Style*. Harlow: Longman.

Lakoff, G. 1987. *Women, Fire and Dangerous Things*. Chicago: University of Chicago Press.

Lakoff, G and Johnson, M. 1980. *Metaphors We Live By*. Chicago: University of Chicago Press.

Whorf, B.L. 1956. *Language, Thought, and Reality: Selected Writings of Benjamin Lee Whorf* (ed. John B. Carroll). Cambridge, Mass.: MIT Press.

Topic sentences are not the only form of signposting available to you. There are further features of language that contribute to the cohesion of written argument. One important feature is **connectivity**, which refers to the words and phrases used to connect one part of a sentence with another, or one sentence with the next.

Exercise 4

Below is a summary of some common types of connective used in written argument, with an explanation of their meaning.

- Which of these can you find in the article?
- Are they being used in the ways suggested in the table?
- Do you feel confident that you could use these in your own argument essays, and in the other forms of writing that you do?

There are some suggestions for answer on this exercise at the back of the book.

Table 5.1   Connectives

Type of connective	Meaning	Examples
additives/alternatives	add/give an alternative	and, or, furthermore, also, in addition, likewise, in other words, that is
adversative	contradict, concede	but, yet, though, however, on the contrary
causal	one idea causes another	so, then, for this reason, consequently, it follows that, as a result, therefore, because
continuatives	please continue to follow the text	well, now, of course

Exercise 5

As well as the connectives you have been tracing, there are other words and phrases that have the function of helping the text hang together. These terms are less about logical relations and more about personal expression. One group of terms helps the reader follow the writer's thinking by pointing explicitly to what the writer is doing. In Exercise 1, the term 'discourse markers' was used, to describe the way that speakers signal what they are going to say. There are written equivalents of these markers. Below are some examples that are used in the article, with an explanation of their meaning. Locate them in the text and check out how they operate.

There are no suggestions for answer on this exercise.

Table 5.2 Discourse markers

Term	Meaning
in particular, particularly	I am going to focus in more detail on something
in order to show this the following, such as, for example to unpick this question	I am going to give you some evidence
clearly	I think I have proved this point
after all	I'm assuming you think this is obvious, too
in fact, the fact that	I'm asserting this as fact
to this extent, in a sense	I'm asserting an idea up to a certain point
you'll have noticed	I hope you have noticed
first . . . second, colon . . . semi-colon	I am putting my ideas in order for you

Exercise 6

Another feature that contributes powerfully to how a writer of argument sounds is that of modality. This refers to the extent to which you put forward the statements in your argument as expressions of absolute truth, or tentative suggestion.

There is a range of terms that can help you to express your ideas without sounding too dogmatic or absolute. These are useful because English is not a subject where issues are cut and dried. For example, look at the following terms:

can, could	it is likely that
perhaps	it seems that, this seems to me
maybe	it appears to be the case
would	some of, in some ways
probably	often, generally, commonly
tend to	sometimes
may	something like
might	this sort/type/kind
in a way	

How many of these can you find in the article?

Explain the function of each example you find: what contribution does it make to the writing style?

There are no suggestions for answer on this exercise.

QUOTING AND REFERENCING

Although you may want to be tentative about expressing a black-and-white judgement, you should not be shy about showcasing your reading via quotation and reference.

It is difficult in examined situations to use lengthy quotations, as these have to be committed to memory, along with any reference details. In coursework contexts, you may also not wish to use up your valuable wordcount in this way. The best strategy is to learn and use a few short phrases which express or sum up some important ideas that you feel are at the centre of an issue or interpretation.

If you do want to use a lengthy quotation, you will need to set it apart from the rest of your text (see extract from Whorf in the article, on page 74). Otherwise, short quotations can be integrated into your writing and marked by using inverted commas and some reference details. Make sure you spell writers' and researchers' names accurately, and don't feel the need to introduce them to your reader. If someone is well known, they need no introduction: so phrases such as 'a writer called Keats' or 'a linguist called Chomsky' are redundant. Use their last name on its own.

Different writers use different conventions for inverted commas, but a frequent system is to use double marks for the actual words of someone in quotation, and single inverted commas for your own nuance meanings: that is, where you want to highlight that a term might have different interpretations, such as 'political correctness'.

You may have noticed that this book doesn't actually follow these conventions. There are ways in which typed text can and does depart from what you do in handwritten work: for example, it is impossible to do handwritten italics with any accuracy. Also, textbooks often adopt a different presentation from that of academic print articles.

In coursework, ideas and expressions you quote from secondary sources need to be acknowledged by bracketed references in your text, then a full reference at the end of your work. Obviously, there will be different expectations of you in examined situations, where you might well be able to quote and acknowledge the author of the quotation, but you may not have the kind of precise references you have to hand in coursework contexts.

Look back at the article to see how referencing works. Journal articles are referenced like this:

author name	_date_	_article title_
Goddard, A.	1996.	'Tall stories: the metaphorical nature of everyday talk', in

title of journal	_volume number_
English in Education,	Vol. 30, No. 2.

Where you are referencing less regular sources, such as magazines, newspapers, lectures and Internet material, you should still be able to supply some basic information of author, date and title, in that order. For Internet sources, you need to give the website address where, for a book source, you would supply the publisher's name.

A list of references means something different from a bibliography. While a bibliography is a list of all the reading that has informed your work generally, a references list shows what you have explicitly referred to in your writing. References are seen as more academic than a general bibliography. If you want to make the most of your reading, find a way to use some brief quotations from the texts you have read, then you can include them in your list of references. All this should remind you of the importance of making notes and keeping good records of your reading in the first place: make use of your PASS notes to keep yourself up to date.

Exercise 7

Go back to the section on trigger words in this chapter. Select one of the questions from there and answer it in the form of an argument essay. Pay attention to the following, which have been covered in this chapter:

- The need to understand the question
- The need to have some content for your argument (use the article provided)
- The need to hold a main line of argument
- The importance of a topic sentence for each paragraph
- Connectives
- The discourse markers that are appropriate for written argument
- Modality
- Quoting and referencing (use the article provided)

SUMMARY

This chapter has helped you to develop the skills you need for writing argument essays. In particular it has looked at:

- Argument triggers
- The structure and style of arguments
- Connectivity in argument
- Modality in argument
- Quoting and referencing

SUGGESTIONS FOR ANSWER

CHAPTER 1, EXERCISE 2

You can see evidence in all these texts of the types of thinking and expression at the core of what we later call 'academic'.

Christopher summarises the result of the class experiments via the kind of generic statements characteristic of scientific discourse. Such discourse typically uses present tense verbs, particularly the verb 'to be', to make statements about the world. Here, Christopher says 'real bricks <u>sink</u>', 'plastic bricks <u>float</u>', 'they float because they <u>are</u> not heavy', 'real bricks <u>are</u> heavy'. He is successfully using discourse that depersonalises and aims to make general, factual comments.

Annie and Kelly are both defining and classifying articles in the world around them. Their writing shows that they are thinking about the similarities and differences in the characteristics of objects. The first text catalogues types of paper in terms of usage: sheets for writing letters on, newspapers for reading about the world, decorated paper for wrapping things in, exercise books. The second text offers us 'things about clothes' – information on where they are worn and what they are made of.

The three texts we have looked at so far show an interesting mixture of styles. In Christopher's writing, there is third person pronoun use ('he', 'she', 'it', 'they'), which is typical of scientific writing and any other writing that wants to be considered objective. Annie uses a first person pronoun ('I', 'we') but chooses the plural term, which is often used in non-fiction writing to suggest 'all of us', 'society', rather than having any personal reference. In contrast, Kelly uses the personal form 'I', but then changes to a more removed style in the last sentence, which, interestingly, introduces some complex words – 'polyester', 'denim', 'cotton', 'acrylic'. Kelly's text reminds us that choosing a particular style and maintaining control of it is no easy task. You could also argue at this point that the most interesting texts often break stylistic rules.

Jonathan's text departs from the others by being more of a procedural text. This is a report, like Christopher's, but where Christopher gives us the result or conclusion of the bricks experiment, Jonathan takes the reader step-by-step through the production of the ice cream. Jonathan shows that he knows there are various sections to his report by demarcating the different activities with a line. His use of 'we' is different from Annie's, as Jonathan's is referring to himself and his classmates.

You could say, as with Kelly's text, that Jonathan departs from a strictly factual account by his use of informal and imaginative language – 'all browny', 'it smelled like ready brek' – and that his text is all the better for breaking the rules. It is worth remembering that any formula for writing should not override a writer's personal voice, and that written genres are dynamic forms of communication that do and should change over time.

It is notable that all these young writers have a keen sense of writing as inseparable from other aspects of visual communication, such as pictures. Although adults tend to classify writing and art forms as different aspects of communication, academic writing often does use graphics – such as charts, tables and figures – to illustrate the verbal text.

Looking at these extracts should have brought home to you that being academic is not a brand new skill to be learnt from now on, rather that academic communication is connected with forms of everyday thinking and expression. These forms need to be identified in your own repertoire, not newly invented.

CHAPTER 1, EXERCISE 4

Logs, Diaries and Reports

Some genres are based on the idea of chronological sequence (a series of events in time). For example, logs, diaries and reports all take the idea of time as their structuring feature. Logs provide a description of what happened each day or in each episode or stage of work; diaries do a similar thing. Sometimes, when assessors ask you to keep a diary rather than a log, the implication is that they have something perhaps more personal in mind. Also, diaries are conventionally divided day by day, with the suggestion that there should be something for you to write every day; logs, on the other hand, might involve extensive notes on one day and nothing for the next month. Sometimes the only difference between a log and a diary is that a Science teacher would be more likely to ask for the first and an English teacher the second. After all, *Star Trek* has 'Captain's log', not 'Captain's diary', while 'Bridget Jones's log' sounds more like a food recipe than a work of fiction.

Reports, while also suggesting coverage of a sequence of events or activities, are more summarising in their function than either logs or diaries. Reports tend to offer an overview, giving the big picture rather than going into every minor detail of occurrences. Think of your end-of-year reports from teaching staff, or the feedback you sometimes get from teachers at the end of assignments: in these cases, there is always an attempt to pick out major points and issues that are thought to run through the work or behaviour under scrutiny.

While writing in note form is often accepted or even expected for diary and log entries, the report tends to be a more formal genre.

Commentaries

While commentaries in sports events are a running account of the action, this is not what is meant in an academic context by this term. What is implied is something more directly analytical, framing a judgement on a text by pointing out its features. On some English courses you write commentaries on your own writing, in which case you need to discuss the choices you made during the writing process.

Short Answers

This genre might appear self-explanatory, but its easy-sounding name hides quite a lot of complexity. Short answers are often asked for on exam papers, occurring when a question is split into various parts. Sometimes such questions involve textual analysis (i.e. asking you to comment on a printed extract), but that is not always the case. Short answers need to pack a lot of information into a small space. The art is to know how much detail to go into, and to be able to assess how the larger question has been sub-divided into distinctive areas, so that you achieve coverage without duplication. This genre is explored further in Chapter 3 of this book.

Research Projects/Investigations

A project or investigation is an extended study where you set up an enquiry into an aspect of an academic subject: for example, English Language, English Literature, English Language and Literature. At the core of this genre is the idea of the writer being active – selecting texts, going out to interview people, recording a conversation – and analysing the material collected. A write-up of a project or investigation is likely to have a number of different sections. This genre is explored more fully in Chapter 4.

Essays

An essay is a setting out of a writer's ideas on a particular topic. It is not based on the idea of following a time sequence, as with logs and diaries, but is organised according to themes. There are many ways to approach this format, and much depends on the instructions you are given in the question. This genre is explored more fully in Chapters 2, 3 and 5.

CHAPTER 2, EXERCISE 4

Questions 1 and 6 start with directions to the reader on how to find the texts for study, and remind the reader to read carefully. These prompts should not be ignored: they are included to make sure you write about the correct text(s), and to signal that any answer must refer closely to those texts.

Question 1 moves from its instruction to read carefully to a direction to the reader to pick out some language features from the passage: 'comment linguistically on' means 'find some examples of language and make sure you say language-oriented things about those features'. As this is a transcript where a regional speaker is reminiscing about his childhood, you could go astray by talking too much about the content of those memories, rather than commenting on such language features as the use of regional forms.

The second bullet point in question 1 moves from the trigger 'comment on' to 'explain'. This is intended to remind you that you should not stop at the level of description – i.e. saying what's there in the passage – but go further and say something about how the language features connect with the messages being conveyed by the speaker: for example, does a dialect feature seem particularly expressive of certain ideas or feelings?; how do features of speech such as hesitancy or repetition connect with what is being expressed at the moment they occur?

Question 2 adds information to the trigger by identifying two areas to target: **verse form** and language use. Although, technically, verse form is a type of language use, the question setter is reminding you that looking at verse form is not the only kind of language use you might focus on. For example, you might look at the formality of the vocabulary, at metaphor – in fact, any aspect of language use that occurs in everyday communication. If the setter had just said *language* as the focus, you might not have realised that this should include verse form.

Questions 3 and 4 both use the trigger 'write about', but couple this term with some very specific instructions on what to focus on. Question 3 asks you to do a textual comparison of dictionary definitions; question 4 asks about narrative structure in a specific chapter. It is only because the instructions which surround 'write about' are so specific that the term is appropriate. You'd be unlikely to find an instruction on its own, such as 'write about this poem'.

Question 5 uses 'consider', while both 6 and 7 use 'discuss'. Question 6 also uses 'comment on'.

In all these examples, the trigger words are heavily modified by detail that points the reader to specific areas. In question 5, 'consider' means 'how': *how* does Jane Gardam make use of children . . .? Outside of a literary context, the question sounds slightly odd, as if some reference is being made to child labour. But what the setter is referring to is 'use' in a literary sense. Writers include references to people and things, not just to represent the real world but in order to stand for ideas and experiences – in other words, as **symbols**.

The trigger 'discuss' in questions 6 and 7 is pinned down to a series of areas in the former and a single one in the latter. 'Comment on' in question 6 reminds candidates that they should refer closely to the specified aspects of the texts. Question 7 uses the trigger 'think of' before the second trigger of 'discuss'. 'Think of' does mean exactly what it says, but it also means, of course 'say what you have thought of'. For the setter, 'think of' is a way of signalling that you should refer to some specific, named situations.

CHAPTER 3, EXERCISE 1

Question 1a

The texts are similar in genre and source. They are both advertisements, and are clearly advertising the same company – the AA. Both texts are promoting a particular part of the company, 'The Driving School', the department that offers driving tuition for learners.

The texts have some content in common: for example, both texts promote the following aspects of the school's provision: discounts and special offers on other AA products if you book tuition; fully qualified instructors; good cars to learn in. There are also similarities in terms of logo style and telephone contact details, although Text B mentions a website too.

> Marks: some fairly basic remarks about content, but relevant, and a good starting point. If you did something like this about content, award yourself 4 marks.

Despite the similarities noted, there are considerable differences. For a start, the adverts' hooklines are very different. Text B uses a strong intertextual message where the line – which, in its full form, would be 'learn to drive' – resembles both a car registration plate and a text message. In contrast, the hook in Text A looks very formal. It is a statement which, although the pronoun 'you' is used, could be read as rather impersonal, meaning 'one school can cover both tests'. 'You' here is the kind of usage that could be read as 'one', an indefinite third person pronoun: 'one only needs'.

> Marks: a good point about intertextuality: give yourself 2 marks for this. For contrasts between hooks, give yourself 2 marks.

The layout and design features of the texts are also very different. Text B features a young woman gleefully tearing up her L-plates. The inference is that the AA have taught her well and so she has passed with flying colours. Interestingly, she is a certain kind of figure: a twenty-something person, casually but neatly dressed, wearing rather conventional jewellery and make-up and no tattoos or body piercings, no revealing necklines, no dark nail varnish. This is a responsible-looking person who, although pictured from above as if to endorse the idea of her as a learner, looks confident and capable. In contrast, Text A uses no image. It does, however, use the graphological strategy of the circled text, where a reader appears to have highlighted an important part of the message. This must be connected with the fact that Text A appeared in *Yellow Pages*, where readers are likely to do just that in reality.

Text A has a leaflet-style layout, which is well ordered with bullet points and firm borders. Text B, in contrast, looks much more messy. The verbal text wraps around the image, and the page has the look of a newspaper or magazine article, with the hookline acting as a headline and the first paragraph emboldened in the style of tabloid news stories.

> Lots of good comments on layout and design: if you got all this, award yourself 10 points.

Although the two texts are similar in content, the way readers are addressed by the narrator is very different. In Text B, the AA refer to themselves as 'we': 'we believe', 'we're the only national driving school', 'we even make learning easy'. The 'you' pronoun in this text is used with a distinct personal reference: 'so you get the best possible tuition', 'you learn in a new Ford Fiesta', 'easy on your pocket'. In contrast, Text A has no use of 'we', the corporate voice. Instead, the narrator refers to the AA's school as if it is a third party: 'the only national driving school to exclusively use . . .'

There are further aspects of grammar that are noticeably different. In Text B, grammatical cohesion is unlike that of formal written texts. For example, several sentences are minor and involve non-standard connectives: 'wherever you live', 'and why you learn', 'and air conditioning'. The effect is to suggest more of a speaker than a writer. This is endorsed by the informal quality of phrases such as 'no wonder'. Text A also has minor sentences, mainly in the form of noun phrases such as 'modern, dual-controlled, tuition car' but these suggest a note-like description which fits the bullet point structure of the information text.

> Marks: lots of good points here about grammar, a tricky area to describe. Important points made about narrative point of view and pronoun usage. 10 marks in total.

Semantically, although both texts obviously concern themselves with driving and thus have similar semantic fields, the emphasis of Text B is on learning, and the vocabulary items reflect that, repeating references to learning several times, from the text message 'lrn' all the way down to the slogan at the bottom, 'first choice for learning'. Each time, a different aspect of learning is emphasised: the pleasure of learning, safety and comfort, cost, and success rates. The piece before the phone number urges the reader to 'book your lessons'. In offering the learning experience, Text B also endorses Ford cars, for obvious reasons.

> Marks: good points about semantics. 6 marks for these.
>
> Possible total so far: 34

Question 1b

The similarities and differences identified above are clearly linked with the different target audiences being appealed to, and the different sources in which the two adverts appeared. Text A's source, the *Yellow Pages*, is a directory aimed at a general readership, while the Ford magazine is likely to be bought by people who are already interested in cars and driving (who perhaps own a car and have children who need driving tuition) or who are young professionals hoping to pass their test and buy a car.

> Marks: discussion of sources – 4 marks for this.

Text A is aiming to be an informative-looking text which presents the strong points of the company in a professional, straightforward and serious way. In *Yellow Pages*, this text would be competing against adverts from rival driving schools, and the AA has gone for a plain and factual presentation. The suggestion is that they don't need fancy names or to make a song and dance about their product because they have a solid reputation which needs simple description rather than a hard sell.

> Marks: summary of nature of presentation to general audience – 6 marks.

Text B goes for a much more fun presentation, connoting youth in its use of text messaging and featuring a young smiling new driver. There is more space available here to develop a story compared with Text A, and the advert uses that space by presenting an informal, speech-like address to the reader using personal pronouns. The message is that learning to drive needn't be difficult, frightening or expensive. The use of a female figure for the image is interesting: perhaps young men are expected to learn to drive, so advertising to them would be a waste of time.

> Marks: summary of nature of presentation to youthful audience – 6 marks.
>
> Maximum possible points: 50.
>
> Refer to 'The Verdict' on page 90.

Question 2a

The first page of any novel is important because it acts like a film trailer to show the flavour of what's coming up. This is, therefore, a challenging task for writers. In this trailer or taster, they have to perform the book in miniature: not only is it a good idea to give the reader a strong sense of space and time (**spatio-temporal point of view**); writers also need to establish the voice of the narrator (**psychological point of view**) and present something of the take on life that will be running through the text (**ideological point of view**). The aim of all this work is to capture the attention of readers and keep them by using forms of language that are interesting and intriguing. Readers have to like the way they are being addressed, or they will not read on.

> Marks: good points on different aspects of point of view. Give yourself 15 if you included these ideas, even if you didn't use the exact terms above.

Question 2b

The first thing that you notice as a reader is how short the chapters are: these two initial chapters only take up a single page. The chapters on page 1 function as episodes where different suspicious incidents are presented, giving us a rapid experience of the theme of the book, a theme which is characteristic of the detective genre as a whole. The rapid scene changes also give us the sense that there are lots of suspicious cases: the arson investigator's caseload is indeed heavy. Interestingly, the idea of criminal fire-setting as an everyday occurrence is much more dramatic than if the narrator had been making a big song and dance about it all.
Less is more, perhaps.

> Marks: good comments about genre (expectations of detective fiction). 5 marks for these.

'Less is more' also applies to some of the grammatical and semantic devices used by the narrator. Short, simple sentences and bald statements of fact have a shocking force which long, complex sentences full of elaborate detail would never have achieved. For example:

> 'Woman's lying in bed and the bed's on fire.'

If this had been something like the following it wouldn't have worked at all:

> 'On the Californian Pacific coast, a woman was lying in bed, apparently asleep, while flames were licking inexorably around the bed and across her body.'

> Marks: grammar (sentence length) – 3 marks. Semantics (level of descriptive detail) – 2 marks.

The brevity of the sentences and their line arrangement make some of the text, at least the first chapter, resemble poetry. In fact, it is difficult to say exactly why the text is prose and not poetry. It is an interesting question, though, why the writer wanted to make his prose look like and sound like poetry. Perhaps it is because we associate poetry with achieving a powerful impact with a few well-chosen words.

Marks: intertextuality and genre – 5 marks.

Both chapters also use a grammatical device which you often see in poetry, and one which also contributes to the idea of dramatic presentation: the use of present tense verbs:

'Woman's lying in bed and the bed's on fire.'

The present tense of a verb, used in a narrative context, is sometimes referred to as the **dramatic present** because it suggests that the events being described are happening now. The present tense also appears in another context, sometimes referred to as *generic*. The **generic present** can suggest a permanent state of affairs that supposedly obtains as a general truth. We use this tense in proverbs ('a stitch in time saves nine'), and in non-fiction texts of all kinds to express facts ('the elephant is a heavy plant-eating mammal'). You saw the use of this feature in the children's writing in Chapter 1.

Marks: grammar again, not an easy aspect to describe – 5 marks.

The idea of the present tense as expressing a removed, general truth as well as expressing an event occurring in real time is relevant to our narrator's presentation, for there is a suggestion of both ideas in the initial scenes. Arson, it seems, is constantly with us, affecting named individuals such as George Scollins, but it is also about countless nameless victims such as 'woman' in the first chapter. It is universal and particular; it is happening now, and always.

The ideas above are held in a delicate balance, and this tells us a lot about the narrator's self-presentation (and then ultimately about the construction of the narratee, or implied reader). If the narrator presented the arson as a shocking drama never before encountered, we would feel that a naïve person was addressing us, and that we were being constructed as naïve too. But if the voice is too world-weary, giving up in the face of the overwhelming prevalence of the crime, what would be the point of any investigation, and therefore what would be the point of the book? Would we, as readers, be prepared to accept reading about a series of crimes that have no chance of being solved?

> Marks: some complex ideas above about point of view – 10 marks.

The balance between investigative zeal and cynicism, energetic attention and cool inattention, is constructed via a range of language devices, of which the use of present tense verbs is only one example. There is a sharpness of detail which suggests the narrator's interest in these scenes; but also a note-like quality implying a business-like detachment; there is a use of everyday idiomatic language, suggesting a kind of casual language user ('flame *licks*'), but such idioms are revealed for what they are, suggesting an uncomfortable critical awareness ('flame licks at her thighs like a lover'); George Scollins's bonfire is not surprising at all, which is why it should merit a particular scrutiny; *California Fire and Life* is just the name of the insurance company, but California fire and life is the world of the book and will be what is contested in all the following pages.

> Marks: good comments on semantics – 5 marks.
> Maximum possible marks: 50.
> Refer to 'The Verdict' below.

The Verdict:

40–50 Excellent

You have a good eye for detail and you are finding many relevant points. You go beyond description to a good level of analysis. You have a wide-ranging, comprehensive approach which will ensure your success. Keep going!

30–40 Very good

You are finding quite a few points but you could go further and say more about them. You may sometimes move away from analysis towards description. Make sure you always ask yourself the 'how' and 'why' questions, not just the 'what' one.

20–30 Average result

You make some good points but you also miss a fair bit. It may be that you are concentrating on too limited an area. Alternatively, you may be covering a lot of ground but doing it too descriptively. See the comment above about 'how' and 'why'.

10–20 Poor result

Your result could be for a range of reasons, including perhaps running out of time. If so, you need to do more timed practice.

Perhaps you just went for the more obvious features, rather than digging around in the text a bit more. If so, organise some prompts for yourself to help you remember some of the terms, concepts and categories that have been used in this exercise.

0–10 Very poor result

You are hardly being analytical at all. You are either paraphrasing the text, not writing enough, or making irrelevant comments – possibly all three. Perhaps you have misunderstood or completely underestimated the task. Go back over the sample answers and list some of the terms, concepts and categories that have been used in the exercise. When you have done this, find a further text and try again. You need to do a lot of practice!

Question 3

The features below are characteristic of the writer's style in this extract. In order to mark your work, or the work of another student, you will need to see how far these techniques have been used in the writing of the piece, and then how far the techniques have been discussed in the commentary.

A marks allocation is given below, first for the writing itself and then for the commentary.

In order to understand the level of achievement you have shown, read 'The Verdict' on page 92.

Own writing

Features	*Marks*
Sparing and careful use of words	8
Poetic-looking layout	4
Present tense verbs	8
Rapid scene change	8
Suggestion of suspicious events	10
Balance between shock and coolness in the way the narrator presents him/herself	12

(To get a fuller picture of the way these features work, read the suggestions for answer for question 2).

Maximum possible marks: 50.

Commentary

Features	*Marks*
Sparing and careful use of words	3
Poetic-looking layout	2

continued

Present tense verbs	3
Rapid scene change	3
Suggestion of suspicious events	3
Balance between shock and coolness in the way the narrator presents him/herself	6

Maximum possible marks: 20.

The Verdict:

a Own writing:

40–50 Excellent

You have a good analytical eye and you realise that a good piece of writing is something you craft carefully after close reference to models. You have been resourceful in using the model you have been given, adapting it creatively.

Keep up the good work!

30–40 Very good

Your performance was sound, but you missed one or two important aspects of the writing style you were asked to model your work on. However, what you did produce worked quite well as a narrative.

20–30 Average result

Your work was uneven, sometimes working well but in the end not following the model you were given closely enough. Perhaps you were not sure how far you were supposed to adopt the style of the original. You need to realise that a model needs to be analysed and followed closely.

10–20 Poor result

Your result could be for a range of reasons, including perhaps running out of time. If so, you need to do more timed practice. Perhaps you used the model text too loosely as a reference point, seeing it simply as a general stimulus. You probably didn't analyse the model text well enough in the first place.

0–10 Very poor result

Your writing had only the vaguest connection with the original model. Perhaps you misunderstood the nature of the task. Go back over the sample analysis of the text and see how that formed the basis for the list of features for writing. Find some further texts to analyse and model your writing on.

You need to do a lot of practice!

b Commentary:

17–20 Excellent

You have put your analytical skills to good use here. You understood the task and have selected significant points perceptively.

13–16 Very good

You have made a range of good analytical points, but you could have gone further in explaining what you were trying to achieve.

9–12 Average result

You have made some good points, but you need to refer more closely to the language features of your text. You are perhaps being too general in your comments, or only giving part of the picture.

5–8 Poor result

Your coverage of points is limited and not sufficiently analytical. Decide whether your problem was the quality of writing you did in your own piece or whether this activity was approached in the wrong way. In either case, go back over the task and see what happened.

0–4 Very poor result

You have perhaps misunderstood the task. Read the sample answer for question 2 in order to see what an analytical approach consists of.

CHAPTER 4, EXERCISE 1

The two texts alone could be the basis of a research question: how does a single company vary its advertising? If you were able to find a further text by the AA (perhaps the homepage of its website), this would add a further interesting variation to the idea of advertising placement.

If you were interested in spoken language, the language of driving tuition would make for a fascinating study, taken just on its own. It would be difficult to compare that with the written texts, because you wouldn't really be comparing like with like. To compare the spoken text with something, you would have to find a driving instruction manual or some written teaching material.

Although speech and writing might not yield a good comparison, you could compare the driving adverts with other genres of written material about driving – for example, a highway code or a driving licence or an extract from a novel. What you would be doing here would be comparing across written genres in order to see how the different purposes of the texts affect the language used.

Written texts might also lend themselves to some interesting historical and/or intercultural comparisons. For example, there are many older versions of the highway code, and different cultures have very different sorts of texts. An American driving licence, for instance, is different from a UK one. Advertising texts which aim to sell cars to different cultural groups are famously different in terms of the aspects they stress (see Goddard 2002).

The intertextual registration plate on one of the AA adverts might have got you thinking about personalised name plates. What forms of language use do you see on these? Are there patterns, where people express particular ideas?

Finally, don't forget TV/film texts and whole novels. For example, there are many different films in the road movie genre, including *Thelma and Louise* and *Crash*; there are also very many novels involving journeys, by car or otherwise. But how do they differ in their narratives and other aspects of language use?

The range of structural or functional aspects of language you choose to cover is of course dependent on what exactly you are analysing. In most cases, though, you will probably need to mention both structures and functions, and say something about how the two systems are linked. To pinpoint a language feature is half the story: saying what a language feature is for – its purpose – is the other half.

Again, the number of social groups you might refer to will depend on what you are doing. Normally, the best advice would be to try to limit the extent of your coverage in order for you to make your investigation manageable. It's difficult to talk about region *and* age *and* gender *and* occupation *and* ethnicity *and* social class without making your work either too complex or too superficial. So go for one big category. You can always mention one or two of the others briefly, to let your reader know that you are aware of them.

CHAPTER 4, EXERCISE 2

When you did the exercise on this opening in Chapter 3, the first task was to think about the work that writers need to do at the beginning of a novel. This extract, of course, is only one example. You could therefore add some further texts for comparison, but drawn from different genres: for example, romantic fiction, horror, science fiction, autobiographical fiction. Your question here would be to explore the extent to which all such writers have a common task, or whether the work of establishing a narrative works differently in different sub-genres of prose fiction.

An alternative exploration which stays with the idea of openings would be to compare adult- and child-oriented fiction in order to see whether writers see the need to do introductory work differently according to the age of their audience.

A further comparison would be to look across different literary genres, for example, prose fiction and drama. Here you might see some very different ways of opening a story, according to the context and traditions that each of the genres has to abide by.

CHAPTER 4, EXERCISE 3

Here are some of the headings you may have devised for your categories. For each, there is an indication of the type of discussion you would be expected to produce.

Source: *Yellow Pages*

Names of places and people

Examples: Gosforth SoM, Bede driving school, Bob Robson SoM, Ken Cooper SoM, Noel's Driving School.

The *Yellow Pages* directory has local variations, and this shows up in some of the place names. For example, Gosforth is an area of Newcastle. People's names also feature strongly in the data. Some of these are famous, others not. Bede is a well known name, being that of a religious figure who lived in Jarrow. Local references may be thought to be attractive because people in a region will often feel pride and interest in their regional identity. A local place name or historical reference may therefore give a sense of security, suggesting that the school has a good, solid pedigree.

Contemporary individuals' names – presumably the names of the founders of the schools – vary in the form in which they appear. Some use first name only, while others use first name plus surname. First name only connotes familiarity and approachability. It's interesting that even where the full names are used, the first name occurs in an abbreviated form. It's also significant that there are no female names.

Positioning

Examples: 1A Passmasters, 1 Ace school of motoring, 1st Ladydrive.

Because *Yellow Pages* list companies alphabetically, there is some usefulness is coming at the front. The first two names above have taken no chances on this, using not only the letter A but also the number 1, to connote excellence twice over. 1st Ladydrive couples the idea of winning with the suggestion that this school might provide female instructors for women who don't want to be taught by a man.

Although the same alphabetical ordering is used in the *Internet Directory*, there does not seem to be such an interest in placement. There are no big visual items, so the pages seem much less busy than those of the *Yellow Pages*.

Play with sound and/or meaning

Examples: EZYPAS SoM, L-Passo, Pass Mark, Drivetime, Driving Force, Green for Go.

Deviant spellings such as 'ezy' are attention-seeking, and this can be a useful strategy where texts are competing with others in a crowded space. Humour in the form of double meanings – as in 'L-Passo' – and the intertextual connotations in phrases such as 'Driving Force' and 'Green for Go' also make readers do extra work on the language in order to tease apart the meanings.

Semantic field of schooling

Examples: Academy Driving School, 1st Choice Quickpass Driving Academy, 1A Passmasters, Pass Mark, Sure Pass Driving School, 1 Ace school of motoring, 1st Ladydrive.

This could be broken down into several sub-areas. For example, some names explicitly mention the terms 'school' and 'academy'. Others refer to success in the tests that are part of any schooling system: for example, 'Sure Pass Driving School'. In other names, the suggestion is that the tuition itself is of an excellent standard, for example, '1 Ace school of motoring'.

Psychological factors

Examples: Calm Drive, Karma school of motoring

Learning to drive is often seen as a nerve-racking experience and so the idea of helping learners to be calm and relaxed has its advantages. There is an interesting question here, though, about whether it is ever advisable to refer to negative aspects in this way, because it could be taken wrongly. For example, you might think that people become hysterical in learning to drive with these companies, forcing the schools to focus on calmness as a reactive remedy.

Source: Internet Directory

The website addresses show some interesting differences from the *Yellow Pages* data. For a start, there are no local references, presumably because websites are not limited by geography so are likely to try for as wide a coverage as possible. The task for website owners is to get people onto their sites by giving themselves the kind of names people might come up with by association. Aside from the British School of Motoring, the addresses use combinations of words and phrases that are in the general semantic field of driving tuition. However, to go for names such as Karma or Ladydrive could lead to confusion with religion or even pornography.

Structurally, the website names look very different, with lower-case type and no spaces. These are conventions that apply generally to Internet addresses.

Here is a possible conclusion to the study:

> In investigating the nature of driving school names, several patterns of linguistic usage were found, with some factors being shared by the two different sources, and others being distinctive to one source. There was more data from *Yellow Pages* than from the *Internet Directory*, so any conclusions on how these names relate to each other must remain tentative.

The *Yellow Pages* data showed certain strategies that could be connected with the way material is organised in such a book: for example, the use of the letter A on the front of names in order to ensure early placement, and the use of attention-seeking strategies such as humour and wordplay in order to compete with rival texts. The semantic field of schooling was prevalent, and there were references to the local and familiar in place names and personal names.

The website addresses also showed use of a general semantic field of driving and learning, but there were no local references. This would make sense for companies who are uncertain where their clientele may be located.

It is interesting that although both sets of data demonstrate some very inventive forms of language use, there is a limit to the kinds of references they supply. There are clear taboos around their wordplay, so it is unlikely, for example, that driving schools would use names such as 'The crash barrier', 'The hard shoulder', 'Jack Knife's SoM', 'Cut U Up', 'Road Hogs Inc'. But perhaps this is a trend that we may see in the future.

CHAPTER 4, EXERCISE 4

Possible categories:
    Grammatical structures: many are two-word noun phrases with no article. This is an example of something that could be tabulated and quantified.

Single word metaphors: *Sidetracked/Aftermath/Freezing/Heartwood*
Music – intertextual references: *Cosi fan Tutti/Let it Bleed/One for the Money*
References to coldness: *Freezing/Cold Light*
Darkness: *Set in Darkness/Dark Lady/Dark Hollow*
Blood: *Blood Work/Blood Rain/Let it Bleed*
Dead and death: *The Big Sleep/Every Dead Thing/How the Dead Live/Known Dead/Dead Lagoon/A Long Line of Dead Men*
Places: *LA Requiem/Dead Lagoon*
Religion: *World Without End/God is a Bullet/Mystic River/The Church of Dead Girls/Prayers for Rain*
Women as victim: *The Concrete Blonde/Church of Dead Girls/Dark Lady*
Weather: *In a Dry Season/Blood Rain/Thin Air/Prayers for Rain/Freezing*

CHAPTER 5, EXERCISE 1

mark my words	mind you	and another thing
so what?	how come?	that's rubbish
it stands to reason	I'm not being funny, but . . .	don't get me wrong, but . . .
to be fair	at the end of the day	it strikes me that
well, if you ask me	I'd just like to say	to my mind

Many of these phrases don't have exact meanings in the way a single word has. This is because they are **discourse markers**, where their meaning arises from what speakers are trying to do in the conversation. For example, 'I'm not being funny, but . . .' and 'don't get me wrong, but . . .' are often used where speakers are about to say something negative and want to cushion it. There is a formal spoken version of these – 'with all due respect . . .'

Some phrases enable speakers to signal that they are about to express an opinion: for example, 'it strikes me that', and 'to my mind'. Others do the same but are stronger expressions, suggesting that the speaker knows they are going to contradict what another has said, for example, 'well, if you ask me' and 'I'd just like to say'.

Some terms are concessionary, used to acknowledge the value of others' points: for example, 'to be fair' and 'mind you'. Others are the opposite, making strong claims for speakers' own positions, for example, 'it stands to reason' and 'mark my words'.

A range of phrases exists for very specific functions. For example, 'and another thing' signals that the list of points will go on; a phrase such as 'that's rubbish' is a dismissive rejection of another's idea; 'so what?' and 'how come?' ask explicitly for explanations.

None of these phrases would work well in formal written argument. This is because they are all based on the idea of interactivity, where the relationship between speakers is as important as the ideas that are being proposed. Although in written arguments the relationship between writer and reader is important, it is not maintained in the immediate way that it is in speech. For this reason, using the terms above would create the wrong **register**.

There are occasional equivalents of these terms in writing, usually resulting in increased formality. For example 'and another thing' could be expressed as 'in addition'. 'That's rubbish' might become 'that doesn't make sense'.

Using questions as part of an argument essay needs to be done carefully. There is a particular type – called a **rhetorical question** – that is often associated with political speeches but which can occur in forms of written persuasion too. Its function is to get the reader or listener to agree with the sentiments of the writer or speaker. Here is an example:

> Shakespeare would have spoken like a Brummie; Keats was a Cockney. So why do people see English Literature as the product of RP-accented, Standard English-users?

For any kind of question to work, you need to control your style of language use well. If you are sometimes not confident about how you sound in writing, you would probably be best advised to avoid them. This is easy to do. Here is another version of the two sentences above, this time avoiding the question form:

Shakespeare would have spoken like a Brummie; Keats was a Cockney. Despite this, people still see English Literature as the product of RP-accented, Standard English-users.

CHAPTER 5, EXERCISE 2

The abstract tells you the article will be arguing that everyday language contains a lot of metaphor, and that this idea has been ignored up to now. It also says that English teachers have been asked to concentrate on literature rather than language in the past, resulting in important areas of study being neglected.

Opening paragraph:
The topic sentence here refers back to the title of the article, then points forward by saying what 'this article' is going to do.

Paragraph 2
The topic sentence links back to the idea of metaphor raised in the second sentence of the opening paragraph.

Paragraph 3
The topic sentence refers explicitly to the metaphorical language used in the previous two paragraphs.

Paragraph 4
The topic sentence continues the connection with metaphor by arguing that the use of everyday metaphor is common, and goes unnoticed.

Paragraph 5
The topic sentence continues with the idea that we don't notice metaphors in everyday language. Then the same sentence says that we do notice metaphors in literature.

Paragraph 6
There is an explicit link to the idea above when the writer says 'this question' (i.e. not noticing everyday expressions, but noticing literary uses). The writer says they are going to 'unpick' the question, which means that the paragraph will explore the issue further.

Paragraph 7
The topic sentence starts with the phrase 'these representations', referring back to the ideas in the previous paragraph. This sentence also points forward by referring to 'a larger picture' which will be discussed.

Paragraph 8
The topic sentence uses the phrase 'these ideas', to refer back to the previous discussion. This paragraph consists of one long sentence, part of which suggests that language and literature are often seen as opposites.

Paragraph 9

The topic sentence starts with the phrase 'through polarisations of this sort', referring back to the opposites mentioned above.

Paragraph 10

The topic sentence starts with 'in the end, though'. This suggests that the writer is going to say something that will link with previous ideas but through slight contradiction or a sense of defeat.

CHAPTER 5, EXERCISE 4

Table 5.4 Examples of connectives in article

Type of connective	Meaning	Examples in article
additives/alternatives	add/give an alternative	and, or, also, in other words, that is
adversative	contradict, concede	but, though, however
causal	one idea causes another	so, then, because
continuatives	please continue to follow the text	well, of course

REFERENCES

Goddard, A. (1996) 'Tall stories: the metaphorical nature of everyday talk', *English in Education*, Vol. 30, No.2.
Goddard, A. (2002) *The Language of Advertising*, London: Routledge.

GLOSSARY

Cohesion   A term which refers to the patterns of language created within a text, mainly within and across sentence boundaries, and which together make up the organisation of larger units of text

Connective   A term to describe words which link linguistic units such as clauses. Words such as 'and', 'but' and 'therefore' are connectives

Developmental   Concerned with the process of learning where easier stages come first and build towards more complex ideas

Discourse markers   Items of language that show the attitude of the speakers or writers to the communication taking place. These can be single words, such as 'briefly', or longer phrases, such as 'to cut a long story short'

Dramatic present   The use of a present tense verb to create immediacy

Expository   Presenting a position, line of argument, or set of views

Focus   The process of homing in on something in detail. This is really a metaphor based on photography: think of adjusting the lens on a camera to get a sharp image

Generic   The ability of a term to refer generally. Generic features are often used in non-fiction to make factual statements and can include particular uses of 'the' and the present tense of the verb 'to be': for example, '<u>the</u> bat see<u>s</u> in the dark'

Generic present   The use of a present tense verb to suggest general truths, for example 'Paris is the capital of France', 'birds have wings'

Genre   A type of text in either speech or writing, for example, recipe, radio programme, poem. Literary genres also refer to different types of literary text, such as fiction, drama and poetry. Within these, there are further categories, such as detective fiction, romantic fiction, etc.

Informants   People who are questioned for research purposes

Modality   Using certain forms of language to express possible conditions. The most frequently used forms for this are **modal verbs**. Examples of modal verbs include 'can', 'may', 'might', 'could', 'would', 'should'

Object   The thing or person on the receiving end of the action expressed by the verb in a sentence. For example, in 'answer the question', 'answer' is the verb and 'the question' is the object

Point of view   As well as meaning 'opinion' or 'belief' in ordinary usage, there is a technical meaning of point of view that refers to narrative structures (stories). Narratives need to establish a **spatio-temporal point of view** (where and when the story takes place), a **psychological point of view** (who is telling the story), and an **ideological point of view** (the attitudes and values assumed by the story)

Procedural   Procedural texts are those that are structured in a step-by-step fashion, such as recipes or DIY instructions

Qualitative   A research approach that values the process of interpretation to determine meaning

Quantitative   A research approach that uses numerical calculations to determine findings

Register   The language that is associated with a particular context and genre, for example, scientific language, casual conversation

Repertoire   A range of styles from which to choose language use for a particular occasion

Rhetorical question   Rhetoric is a term which broadly describes persuasive language, so a rhetorical question is part of a persuasive technique where a speaker deliberately asks a question which is not open-ended

Scope   The range of items that an individual will pay attention to

Symbol   This involves association between things rather than direct reference. For example, a rose or heart can symbolise love

Thematic   Thematic texts are ordered by the grouping together of ideas. This is a different structure from that used by narrative, which is based on time sequences where one event follows another

Topic sentence The first sentence of a paragraph, and the place where the topic of the text is maintained

Verse form The type of verse structure used in a poem, for example, rhyming couplets, sonnet, haiku